Lamek Ronoh

Security Concern of Cloud Computing Models

Lamek Ronoh

Security Concern of Cloud Computing Models

Cloud Service Delivery Models(SaaS,PaaS,IaaS) Vs Deployment Models(Private,Public, Hybrid & Community Clouds)

LAP LAMBERT Academic Publishing

Publisher:
LAP LAMBERT Academic Publishing
is a trademark of
International Book Market Service Ltd., member of OmniScriptum Publishing Group
17 Meldrum Street, Beau Bassin 71504, Mauritius

ISBN: 978-3-659-45243-7

Zugl. / Approved by: Eldoret, Kisii University, 2013

DEDICATION

I dedicate this book to my wife Elseba and our sons Reuel and Levy for the entire support they accorded me while I was working on this scholarly task. To all my friends and colleagues for their invaluable ideas without which this book would not have been completed successfully, to my enemies and detractors for making life worth living.

ACKNOWLEDGEMENT

I wish to acknowledge a number of people who made it possible for this book to be completed. I wish to thank Kisii university for granting me a chance to study in the institution. I sincerely wish to thank my able supervisors Dr. Raymond Ongus and Mr. John Oredo for the time and energy devoted to this work, their invaluable analysis of the work, patience and encouragement brought hope when the situation almost looked hopeless. All those whose names are not mentioned and made contributions to this study. I wish to thank you. May almighty father bless you abundantly!

TABLE OF CONTENTS

LIST OF FIGURES

LIST OF TABLES

LIST OF ABBREVIATIONS AND ACRONYMS

API - Application Programming Interface

ASP - Application Service Provider

DoS - Denial of Service

IaaS - Infrastructure as a Service

ICT – Information and Communication Technology

IP - Internet Protocol

IT - Information Technology

MITM - Man-In-The Middle

MTA - Multi-tenancy architecture

NIDS - Network Intrusion Detection System

NIPS - Network Intrusion Prevention System

NIST - National Institute of Standards and Technology

PaaS - Platform as a Service

SaaS - Software as a Service

SLA - Service Level Agreement

SLO - Service Level Objective

SOA- Service Oriented Architecture

SPSS- Statistics Package for Social Sciences

SSL - Secure Socket Layer

TTP - Trusted Third Party

VM - Virtual Machine

XML - Extensible Markup Language

CHAPTER ONE

INTRODUCTION

1.1 Background of the Study

Innovations are necessary to ride the inevitable tide of change. Most of the enterprises are striving to reduce their computing cost through the means of virtualization. This demand of reducing the computing cost has led to the innovation of cloud computing. Cloud computing offers better computing through improved utilization and reduced administration and infrastructure costs. Cloud computing is a natural evolution of the widespread adoption of virtualization, service-oriented architecture and utility computing. In Kenya, cloud computing is still at infant stage. Therefore, most of the enterprises are not very confident to adopt it. Cloud computing has become one of the most talked about technologies in recent times and has got a lot of attention from media, as well as analysts because of the opportunities it is offers. It has been estimated that the cost advantages of cloud computing to be three to five times for business applications and more than five times for consumer applications (Boss et al., 2007).

In essence, cloud computing is the use of Internet-based technologies for the provision of services, originating from the cloud as a metaphor for the Internet, based on depictions in computer network diagrams to abstract the complex infrastructure it conceals. It offers the illusion of infinite computing resources available on demand, with the elimination of upfront commitment from users, and payment for the use of computing resources on a short-term basis as needed. Furthermore, it does not require the node providing a service to be present once its service is deployed. It is being promoted as the cutting-edge of scalable web application development, in which dynamically scalable and often virtualised resources are provided as a service over the internet, with users having no knowledge of, expertise in, or control over the technology infrastructure of the cloud supporting them. There have been rapid growths in cloud computing adoption by enterprises users for the hosting of data and deployment of services over the past few years and this trend is expected to continue where most firms here in Kenya are expected join and explore its services. (Datapipe, 2010).

Before any organizations jump onto the cloud computing bandwagon, certain inherent issues need to be understood. Customer data security is the top most issue in cloud computing. Failure to thoroughly analyse the risks involved and taking measures to safeguard the company's most valuable asset on the cloud – company data, could have direct and indirect impacts to the business. The impacts could range from direct loss of company's intellect properties to indirect loss of reputation that will ultimately affect the companies' bottom line. Many smaller companies may not survive such an impact. As cloud computing services are increasingly used for processing confidential data, in application like e-commerce website and back-end office accounting system, the security and privacy implication are high should there be a lapse in the security processes (Shinder, 2011).

This study aimed at investigating and analysing subterranean security issues threatening the cloud computing service delivery models namely the Software as a Service (SaaS), Platform as a Service (PaaS) and Infrastructure as a Service (IaaS) and their respective deployment models(Private, public, community and hybrid). The research highlighted latent factors existing in these service delivery models that could be accounting for the variation in security of cloud computing architecture. Variables associated with each of these factors influence the security of data and information in the cloud either positively or negatively. However, their combined effect may results in a significant disparity in the level of security amongst the different cloud computing service and deployment models. This disparity probably may exists because of a variety of factors, which are presented in this study. Thus this research book revolved on cloud computing security concerns notably on service delivery models, a comparative study of selected firms in Kenya.

1.2 Statement of the Problem

With the inception of cloud computing services, it has been believed that the service models namely the Software as a Service(SaaS), Platform as a Service(PaaS) and Infrastructure as a Service(IaaS) together with the type of deployment models namely the public, private, community and hybrid have a significant effect on the security of cloud computing services in general . However, no endeavors have been done to show whether these factors are statistically significant or not. The purpose of this study was to compare security concerns of cloud computing service delivery models and their

2

respective deployment models. More specifically, this study sought to answer the following questions:

i) What are the most critical cloud computing security concerns in SaaS service delivery model and the respective deployment models in the selected firms in Kenya?

ii) What are the most critical cloud computing security concerns in PaaS service delivery model and the respective deployment in the selected firms in Kenya?

iii) What are the most critical cloud computing security concerns in IaaS service delivery model and the respective deployment models in the selected firms in Kenya? In essence, the research problem was to investigate security concerns of cloud computing service delivery models by comparing selected companies in Kenya.

1.3 Objectives of the study

The general objective of the study was to compare the security concerns of cloud computing service delivery models in selected firms in Kenya.

The Specific objectives of the study were:

i) To establish whether SaaS service delivery model and the respective deployment models used have a significant effect on cloud computing security in the selected firms in Kenya.

ii) To establish whether PaaS service delivery model and the respective deployment models used have a significant effect on cloud computing security in the selected firms in Kenya.

iii) To establish whether IaaS service delivery model and the respective deployment models used have a significant effect on cloud computing security in the selected firms in Kenya.

1.4 Research hypotheses

The hypotheses for the study were stated as follows:

i. SaaS service delivery model and the respective deployment models used have no significant effect on cloud computing security in the selected firms in Kenya.

ii. PaaS service delivery model and the respective deployment models used have no significant effect on cloud computing security in the selected firms in Kenya.

iii. IaaS service delivery model and the respective deployment models used have no significant effect on cloud computing security in the selected firms in Kenya.

3

1.5 Justification of the study

The study would benefit companies that have adopted or intend to embrace cloud computing by providing them with a new perspective of looking at security concerns in the cloud. This way, the management of cloud service providers and its clients will be able to make sound decision based on the findings of this research alongside the existing security concerns. This is because the findings would provide the stakeholders in the field of cloud computing and other related technologies a concrete understanding of security concerns for different service delivery models and their respective deployment models.

Thus the justification of the study lies in the fact that with the installation of fibre optic cables and Government plans of putting up and ICT park infrastructure at Konza City, most firms in Kenya are expected to embrace cloud computing sooner or later. It is against this backdrop therefore that serious security policy framework and technical action need to be put in place not only from top management but also from consumers. This study is therefore significant in that it highlighted the pertinent underlying issues that could be determinants of cloud computing security concerns specifically on service delivery models and the respective deployment models. Recommendations has been made in this study which is hoped to help the strategic/tactical management level of Kenya's business enterprises and other stakeholders in adopting cloud computing while putting security concerns into considerations.

1.6 Assumptions of the Study

In this study, it is assumed that:

i) Normality of observations - the population from which samples was drawn is assumed to be normally distributed.

ii) Observations are independently distributed.

iii) Homogeneity: Homogeneity means that the variance of the variables is approximately equal, that is , Variance(δ^2) is constant.

iv) Intervening factors such as legal framework and regulations, tax regimes and company policies were put into consideration.

4

1.7 Scope and limitations of the study

The study was conducted in two selected companies in the Kenya namely the IonaCloud and KenyanCloud. These companies have all the service delivery and deployment models of cloud computing. This study utilized questionnaire that were issued separately to the sampled employees and clients of the said companies. This study was limited in scope to identifying security risks in cloud computing delivery models and their respective deployment models and did not therefore endeavor seek to study security risks of all the other cloud computing services.

1.8 Operational Definition of terms

Cloud computing: Cloud computing is a model that enables convenient, on-demand self-service network access to a shared pool of configurable computing resources such as networks, servers, storage, applications that can be rapidly provisioned and released with minimal management effort or service provider's interaction over the internet infrastructure.

Service delivery models: Also called SPI (SaaS, PaaS and IaaS) model, refers to how cloud computing pooled resources can be delivered to the users on the cloud.

Software as Service (SaaS): This is a capability in which the consumer can use the provider's applications running on the cloud. SaaS is a software distribution model in which applications are hosted by a vendor or service provider and made available to customers over a network, typically the Internet.

Platform as Service (Paas): In this type of service, the consumer can deploy, the consumer created or acquired applications created by using programming languages or tools made available by provider on the cloud infrastructure. Thus PaaS is a model that provides a development platform for the developers and associated services over the Internet without downloads or installation.

Infrastructure as Service(IaaS): This is a capability provided to the consumer by which, it can provision processing, storage, networks and other fundamental computing resources where the consumers can deploy and run the software e.g. operating systems, application programs etc. IaaS involves outsourcing the equipment used to support operations, including storage, hardware, servers and networking components- provides a virtualized computer infrastructure.

5

Deployment models: Is a term used to refer to how cloud computing pooled resources are arranged and supplied to the consumers on the cloud. The deployment models comprise of public, private, community and hybrid clouds.

Public Cloud: Is a cloud infrastructure that is available to the general public via the public Internet owned by an organization offering the cloud service available in a "pay as you go" manner to the public.

Private Cloud : The type of the cloud, that is available solely for a single organization or to a select group of customers. This could be managed by an organization or third party and might have been available on premise or off premise. Services are not made available for public.

Community Cloud: In this type of cloud deployment model, the infrastructure of the cloud is shared by several organizations or particular community of users that support a society that has shared common interest for its policy and compliance, mission and vision, security and other relative considerations.

Hybrid Cloud : This is a cloud infrastructure that is a combination of more than one cloud deployment models such as private, community or public. It enables ease of data and application portability and load balancing between clouds.

Hypervisor: A controller popularly known as virtual machine manager (VMM) that allows multiple operating systems to be run on a system at a time, providing the resources to each operating system such that they do not interfere with each other.

Virtualization: Refers to providing an environment that is able to render all the services, supported by a hardware that can be observed on a personal computer, to the end users . The three existing forms of virtualization categorized as server virtualization, storage virtualization and network virtualization.

Security: Security refers to the set of procedures, processes and standards designed to provide information security assurance in a cloud computing environment.

Security concerns: Security concerns encompasses a broad range of security constraints from an end-user and cloud provider's perspective, where the end-user will primarily will be concerned with the provider's security policy, how and where their data is stored and who has access to that data. It comprises of the physical security of the infrastructure and the access control mechanism of cloud assets, to the execution and maintenance of security policy.

CHAPTER TWO
LITERATURE REVIEW

2.1 Theoretical Framework

Cloud computing is a latest buzz in information technology era which shifts computing resources and data away from traditional back-end servers on to data centers. Basically applications, storages, databases and various IT services are delivered as a service over the Internet (Dikaiakos et al, 2009). In a cloud computing environment, the entire data resides over a set of networked resources, enabling the data to be accessed through virtual machines. Since these data-centres may be located in any part of the world beyond the reach and control of users, there are multifarious security and privacy challenges that need to be understood and addressed. There are various issues that need to be addressed with respect to security and privacy in a cloud computing environment (Morsy et al, 2010).

2.1.1 Cloud Computing Architecture

National Institute of Standards and Technology (NIST) is a well accepted institution all over the world for their work in the field of information technology. NIST defines the cloud computing architecture by describing five essential characteristics, three cloud services models and four cloud deployment models (Rehan S, 2011) as depicted in Figure 2.1 below.

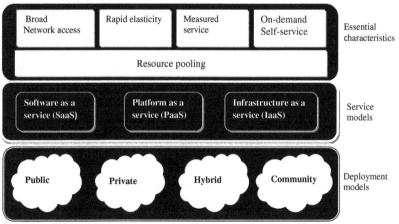

Figure 2.1: Cloud computing architecture
Source: *NIST (2011).*

7

2.1.2 Essential Characteristics of Cloud Computing

As depicted in Figure 2.1 above, there are five essential characteristics of Cloud Computing which explains their relation and difference from the traditional computing. These include:

(i) On-demand-self-service

This service enables customers to provision or un-provision computing resources such as servers, and storages as needed dynamically without interaction from cloud service provider's support. It enables service provider to dynamically assign and reassign services according to customer preference (Mell & Grance, 2011).

(ii) Broad Network Access

It is a web-based user interface that is accessible through standard mechanism from anywhere via Internet/network. Services are also available through heterogeneous thick or thin client platforms such as mobile phone, laptop/tablets, PDA's etc (Savu, 2011).

(iii) Resource Pooling

The computing resources of the provider are pooled to serve multiple consumers which are using a multi-tenant model consisting of various physical and virtual resources dynamically assigned, depending on consumer demand. Examples are storages, processing (CPU) power, memory, virtual machines and network bandwidth resources. Service provider's computing resources are location independent, i.e. customer has no idea or control over the precise location of its data and computing resources (Shinder, 2011).

(iv) Rapid Elasticity

Here, Services are delivered rapidly and elastically provisioned, capable of quick scale out or in for any service or release provisioning. For the customer these capacities often appears to be unlimited and able to purchase in any amount at any time (Rehan S, 2011).

8

(v) Measured Service

Cloud Computing systems automatically control and optimize resource usage by providing a metering capability to the type of services e.g. Storage, processing, Internet bandwidth, or active user accounts. Resource utilization can be checked, measured, limit and reported thus providing clarity for both the service provider and customer of the consumed service (Savu, 2011).

2.1.3 Cloud Service Delivery Models

There are three Cloud Services Models and these three fundamental classifications are often referred to as "SPI model" i.e. software, platform or infrastructure as a service .

(i) Software as Service (SaaS)

This is a capability in which the consumer can use the provider's applications running on the cloud. SaaS is a software distribution model in which applications are hosted by a vendor or service provider and made available to customers over a network, typically the Internet (Smith, 2011).

(ii) Platform as Service (Paas)

In this type of service, the consumer can deploy, the consumer created or acquired applications created by using programming languages or tools made available by provider on the cloud infrastructure. Thus PaaS is a model that provides a development platform for the developers and associated services over the Internet without downloads or installation (Rehan S, 2011).

(iii) Infrastructure as Service

This is a capability provided to the consumer by which, it can provision processing, storage, networks and other fundamental computing resources where the consumers can deploy and run the software e.g. operating systems, application programs etc. IaaS involves outsourcing the equipment used to support operations, including storage, hardware, servers and networking components- provides a virtualized computer infrastructure (Smith, 2011).

2.1.4 Cloud Deployment Models

(i) Public Cloud

Is a cloud infrastructure that is available to the general public via the public Internet owned by an organization offering the cloud service available in a "pay as you go" manner to the public (Savu, 2011).

(ii) Private Cloud

The type of the cloud, that is available solely for a single organization or to a select group of customers. This could be managed by an organization or third party and might have been available on premise or off premise. Services are not made available for public (Thibodeau, 2011).

(iii) Community Cloud

In this type of cloud deployment model, the infrastructure of the cloud is shared by several organizations or particular community of users that support a society that has shared common interest for its policy and compliance, mission and vision, security and other relative considerations (Savu, 2011).

(iv) Hybrid Cloud

This is a cloud infrastructure that is a combination of more than one cloud deployment models such as private, community or public. It enables ease of data and application portability and load balancing between clouds (Rehan S, 2011)

2.2 Cloud Service Models and its security risks

The virtualization technologies is a core technology behind cloud infrastructures. Virtualization provides flexibility to move virtual machines in any location for resource optimization, thus it creates challenge to enforce organization's security and compliance policy since customers are uncertain of the actual physical location of the data and computing resources. Given that the cloud services can be delivered in many flavors, that is, in any combination of service delivery models, SaaS, PaaS and IaaS (SPI), and operational models, public, private and hybrid, the cloud security concerns and solutions are context (pattern) dependent. Hence, the solution architecture should match these concerns and build security safeguards (controls) into the cloud application architecture (Kajiyama, 2012). As mentioned elsewhere in this research study, cloud service models are classified as 'Software-as-a-Service' (SaaS), 'Platform-as-a-service' (PaaS) and 'Infrastructure-as-a-Service' (IaaS). Enterprises should be considering the differences as well as its similarities among these three classifications despite many overlapping areas.

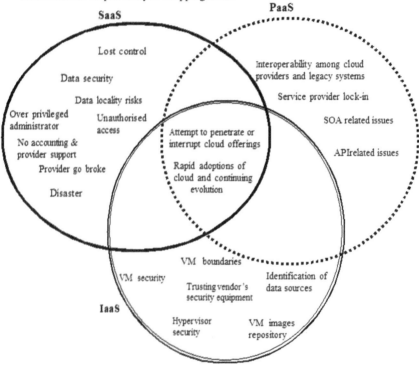

Figure 2.2: SPI risk models
Source: *Thibodeau (2010)*

As shown in Figure 2.2 above, all cloud computing risk were identified and grouped into the three cloud computing model of SaaS, PaaS and IaaS. There were two risks identified to be common for all the three models. They are the rapid adoption and evolution of cloud computing and the increasing risk of cloud computing being targeted by the hackers. The main reason being that cloud computing is dynamic and is constantly changing. Changes in the technology as well as changes in the process make it vulnerable to hacking and policy maker have to keep pace with this changes to come out with the regulation.

2.2.1 Security Risks in SaaS Model

This particular service model provides access to applications which runs on a service provider infrastructure. Services are available from many different client devices via various methods such as a web browser and mobile app. Examples are web-based email and video conferencing. Here the customer does not control or manage underlying IT infrastructure (Thibodeau, 2010). Possible security issues in SaaS model among others include:

(i) Sole dependencies on vendor security model

Customers are solely depending on cloud service provider security measures and standard. Since cloud provider in SaaS supports large number of users, it is hard to make sure that appropriate security measures are taken into the consideration to protect customer data and at the same time, also ensure that the customer application is available with proper security when needed. (Brodkin, 2008).

(ii) Security on the network

Customers are unable to have true picture on the cloud provider systems and network security behind their slick marketing. Hackers can exploit weakness in network security sniffing the packets. Possible threats are Man-In-The Middle (MITM) attack, network penetration, session management weakness and insecure Secure Socket Layer (SSL) trust settings (Morsy, Grundy & Muller, 2010).

(iii) Data security

Hackers can manipulate weakness in data security model to get an illegitimate access to data or application. SaaS are vulnerable for improper access control, virtual machines operating system flaws, cookies and hidden field manipulation as well as insecure storages and configurations (Morsy et al., 2010).

(iv) Identity control

Due to large customers base and verities service type supports by the cloud powder, it is another difficult tasks in cloud environment and mismanagement of identity control may lead to unauthorised data access. Passwords management are also complex and becoming less efficient because hackers now has the readily available tools over cloud and computing capacity to bust through password protections (Smith, 2011).

(v) Data isolation

Encryption maybe helpful in segregating different users' data alongside with other customers in shared environment but it is not an effective cure. Mismanagement (loss of key) of encrypted data can make data totally unusable, and hinter availability of the encrypted data. Beside this, it is difficult to controls or outline administrative tasks between client and cloud provider as often they often need to work together to accomplish certain task. Active third party liabilities protections are also very important because of the amount of data the cloud providers handle make screening quite impossible (Brodkin, 2008).

(vi) Data locality risks

In a cloud customer data may not be physically stored in a source country, perhaps data will be distributed or stored beyond the border thus international data privacy protections and export restriction law may apply and also increase chances of data leaks due to poor security in different geographic (Subra, 2011).

(vii) Privileged user access

Confidential data processed outside the organisation causes an inherent level of risks, as off-shore services bypass the "physical, logical and personnel controls" of IT management over in-house applications (Brodkin, 2008).

(viii) Data integrity

It is difficult to maintain data integrity over distributed infrastructure like cloud computing. In SaaS, applications are multi-tenant hosted by 3rd party thus it usually exposes functionality via Extensible Markup Language (XML) based application Program Interface (APIs). Improper integrity controls at the data level (directly access database bypassing application logic) could result multifaceted security issues (Morsy et al., 2010).

(ix) Disaster

Recovery, since system images are being backed-up and distribute or replicate between multiple sites, it is difficult to do a system recovery when lacking of proper procedure and support from cloud vendor Disaster recovery process could jeopardise the security of the customer's data (Brodkin, 2008).

2.2.2 Security risks in PaaS Model

In PaaS model, service provider provides a platform for customer (developer) to develop and deploy their own or acquired applications. Often service provider provides application programming interface (API) or template based development engine to build custom application. Customer does not manage or control the infrastructure such as servers, network, operating system except deployed applications and its configuration. This service free-up programmers or IT professionals from the complexity of managing own IT infrastructure. PaaS is also vulnerable to most of the SaaS model vulnerabilities discussed above. Possible specific security risks in PaaS are:

(i) Absence of interoperability among cloud providers and legacy systems

Different cloud provider uses different type of security products and methods to secure their infrastructure and legacy stem may have their own backward security protocol thus integration among these pose a security risk and challenge (CCIA, 2009).

(ii) Service provider lock-in

Various cloud providers design their cloud service using their proprietary technology and use security standard or protocol proprietary to their own platform. For an example, Microsoft Azure platform is built on .net and if customer needs to move from Microsoft to some open source platform provided by other vendors, it would be challenging and also the migration process may cause security issues. Therefore it is difficult to move from one provider to another. This scenario could exist in SaaS model as well (Shinder, 2011).

(iii) Service Oriented Architecture(SOA) related issues

PaaS service model is built on Service Oriented Architecture (SOA) model thus it inherits security issues which exists in SOA model such as DoS attacks, MITM and XML related attacks, dictionary attacks, replay attacks, SQL injection attacks and data entry validation related attacks (Shinder, 2011). SOA threats are also available in SaaS model.

(iv) API related issues

If the application programming interface (API) that the customer used to manage and interact with cloud services is not secured, it could the result in sending data in the clear text and that could cause security breach. Different API cloud vendors are using different type of API standard. Applications created with much different type of APIs could create potential security risks due to incompatibility and integration issues (Morsy et al., 2010).

2.2.3: Security Risks IaaS Model

This capability provided to the customer is often refers to as "everything-as-a-service". Generally it represents entire virtual infrastructure as a service over the Internet (includes firewall, RAM, CPU. Purpose of this offering is to replace a customer's server room and network through virtualization technology and it also contributes to cost reduction and improved flexibility. Major players include Amazon, Rackspace, Savvis, HP, IBM, Sun and Google (Thibodeau, 2010). Possible security risks are:

(i) Trusting provider underlying security equipments

It is difficult for cloud customers to fully understand the provider security configuration in core physical level and also ensuring that the service provider configuration standard does not conflict with customer own organizations security policy (CCIA, 2009).

(ii) Identification of appropriate data sources

It is a challenge to determine which data sources are relevant for incident detection particularly with IaaS (providing intrusion detection for virtual machines without knowing installed operating system) and Paas (providing intrusion detection for web applications without knowing the type of applications hosted) (Morsy et al., 2010).

(iii) Virtual Machine (VM) security

Malware, viruses, DOS, memory leaks and other VM operating system and various workloads are most common security threats. The VM's security is a part of customer responsibility in IaaS (Morsy et al., 2010).

(iv) Security in VM images repository

Unlike physical server, VMs image are still under risk when it is in offline. It is common practice to take a snapshot of VMs for disaster recovery. Thus VM images can be under the risk of malicious codes injection when offline and these VM files could be stolen too. Although customer is ultimate responsible for the VM security but since vendor is an owner of the physical hardware there is possibility that cloud provider may copy existing customers VM and reuse for other customer. Another issue in the VM environment is related to VM templates, it is common practice to use template for rapid deployment of system and all these templates may contain the original owner information which may be re-used for new customers (Savu, 2011).

(v) Virtual network security

In IaaS, cloud customers share provider physical infrastructure with many different customers and that increase the risk level of exploiting vulnerabilities in different servers running DHCP, DNS and IP protocols. Virtual Switches (vSwitch) used in IaaS to provide network access to the customer could also be attacked (Morsy et al., 2010).

(vi) Securing VM boundaries

 VM servers can be designed with virtual boundaries (isolated from other VMs) to provide network connectivity among VM servers for security. Generally VMs co-exist in a physical server to share CPU, memory, network card and other resources. Securing VM boundaries fallen under cloud provider responsibility thus misconfiguration and mismanagement could lead unauthorized access and data leaks (NIST, 2009).

(vii) Hypervisor security

Hypervisor is a 'virtualizer' which map physical server to virtual server. It acts as a central medium of any access to the physical server resources by VMs Therefore, any compromise on hypervisor means a compromised hosted VMs. Cloud service provider provides the security of the hypervisor and any vulnerability in hypervisor software inherits security risk in customer VMs (Morsy et al., 2010).

2.3 Review of previous studies

As discussed earlier in this study, the cloud computing utilizes different delivery models, for the different types of cloud computing services delivered to the end user. These models provides the software, platform and hardware using different deployment models namely the Software as service (SaaS), Platform as service (PaaS), and Infrastructure as service (IaaS). The security level is different according to the typed service delivery model used. It against this backdrop that this study was based on the on risks associated with three cloud computing service delivery models when hosted in any of the four deployment models namely the public, private, community and hybrid.

Subashini and Kavitha (2010) conducted a survey of different security risks that pose a threat to the cloud computing. More specifically, their study objectives concentrated towards the issues related to the service delivery models. Their initial architectural findings indicated that IaaS is the foundation of all cloud services, with PaaS built upon it and SaaS in turn built upon it. They argued that, just as capabilities are inherited, so are the information security issues and risks and that there are significant trade-offs to each model in the terms of integrated features, complexity versus extensibility and security. If the cloud service provider takes care of only the security at the lower part of the security architecture, the consumers become more responsible for implementing and managing the security capabilities. These fundamental elements of the cloud require security which depends and varies with respect to the deployment model that is used, the way by which it is delivered and the character it exhibits. Some of the fundamental security challenges are data storage security, data transmission security, application security and security related to third-party resources. This is confirmed by Kandukuri et al (as cited by Subashini, 2009) that guaranteeing the security of data in the cloud is difficult, if not impossible because services are provided on different services delivery models (SaaS, PaaS and IaaS) and that each delivery model has its own security issues. In a nutshell, their research findings pertaining cloud computing risks were presented in threefold. The first findings concentrated on SaaS delivery model which indicated that in SaaS, the client depends on the provider for proper security measures and consequently, the provider must do the work to keep multiple users' from seeing each other's data, which becomes difficult to the user to ensure that right security measures are in place

17

and also difficult to get assurance that the application will be available when needed. This was lent by CCIA (2009) by outlined that any vulnerability at the lower level might have effect in higher level service model. For examples vulnerability in IaaS (hardware firmware level) could lead to security risk at the PaaS and SaaS. Similarly, PaaS model risk (erroneous codes or API) would pose security risk at the SaaS model. They concluded their research on SaaS delivery models by isolating various key security elements as integral part of the SaaS application development and deployment process that should be carefully considered. These elements comprised of data security, network security, data locality, data integrity, data segregation, data access, authentication and authorization. They wrapped up on SaaS security issues findings by suggesting that this security module should cater to all the issues arising from all directions of the cloud and every element in the cloud should be analyzed at the macro and micro level and an integrated solution must be designed and deployed in the cloud to attract and enthrall the potential consumers. Until then, cloud environment will remain cloudy. Secondly regarding PaaS delivery model, Subashini and Kavita(2010) made a rejoinder in their findings that since PaaS delivery model is more extensible than SaaS, it has tradeoffs which extends to security features and capabilities. Among the direct application, security specific metrics available are vulnerability scores and patch coverage. Hackers are likely to attack visible code, including but not limited to code running in user context. They are likely to attack the infrastructure and perform extensive black box testing. The vulnerabilities of cloud are not only associated with the web applications but also vulnerabilities associated with the machine-to-machine Service Oriented Architecture (SOA) applications, which are increasingly being deployed in the cloud. They concluded by suggesting that metrics should be in place to assess the effectiveness of the application security programs and that these metrics can indicate the quality of application coding. Finally, Subashini and Kavita (2010) concluded their study on IaaS delivery model. They became more specific that IaaS is prone to various degrees of security issues based on the loud deployment model through which it is being delivered. In particular, they mentioned public cloud as the one that poses the major risk whereas private cloud seems to have lesser impact. Due to the growing virtualization of 'everything' in information society, retaining the ultimate control over data to the owner of data regardless of its physical location will become a topic of utmost interest. In a conclusive rejoinder, Descher et al (as cited in Subashini and Kavita,

18

2009) advised that in order to achieve maximum trust and security on a cloud resource, several techniques would have to be applied. But his advice was vague because it was not specific to any security technique that can be employed.

In summary, Subashini and Kavita study gave a new perspective of how to view the security issues in service delivery models of cloud computing but it failed to highlight the impact of security issues or concerns of the aforementioned service delivery models when hosted on any of the four cloud computing delivery models namely the private, public, community and hybrid clouds.

Another similar research on cloud computing delivery models was carried by O'Neill (2011). In his study of *"SaaS, PaaS, and IaaS: A security checklist for cloud models"*, he was categorical that when an organization is considering cloud security it should consider both the differences and similarities between the three segments of cloud models. His precautionary findings are as depicted in Figure 2.3(a).

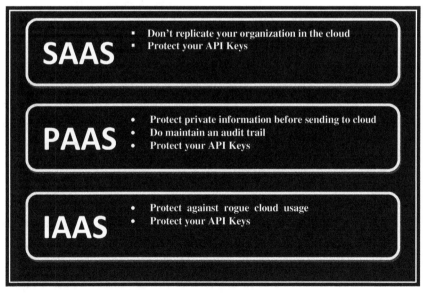

Figure 2.3(a): Security Checklist for cloud delivery models.
Source: O'Neill *(2011)*

Regarding SaaS, O'Neill (2011) advises that we should not replicate one's organization in the cloud because many users with multiple passwords are a potential security threat and a drain on IT help desk resources. The risks and costs associated with multiple passwords are particularly relevant for any large organization making its first foray into cloud computing and leveraging applications or SaaS. For example, if an organization has 10,000 employees, it is very costly to have the IT department assign new passwords to access Cloud Services for each individual user. He gave another example that when the user forgets their password for the SaaS service, and resets it, they now have an extra password to take care of. He summarized his findings on SaaS delivery model by concluding that the danger of not having a single sign-on for the Cloud is increased exposure to security risks and the potential for increased IT help desk costs, as well the danger of dangling accounts after users leave the organizations, which are open to rogue usage. Concerning PaaS, O'Neill (2011) found out that the primary focus of this delivery model is on protecting data before sending it to the cloud. First, he advises that an important element to consider within PaaS is the ability to plan against the possibility of an outage from a cloud provider. The security operation needs to consider providing for the ability to load balance across providers to ensure fail over of services in the event of an outage. Secondly, another key consideration should be the ability to encrypt the data whilst stored on a third-party platform and to be aware of the regulatory issues that may apply to data availability in different geographies. Finally, audit trails on PaaS to be in place because it provides valuable information about how an organization's employees are interacting with specific Cloud services, legitimately or otherwise. Finally, pertaining IaaS, O'Neill (2011) recommends that IaaS should be protected from rogue cloud usage, the main focus being management of virtual machines. The chief security officers priority is to overlay a governance framework to enable the organization to put controls in place regarding how virtual machines are created and spun down thus avoiding uncontrolled access and potential costly wastage. The classic use case for governance in cloud Computing is when an organization wants to prevent rogue employees from misusing a service. For example, the organization may want to ensure that a user working in sales can only access specific leads and does not have access to other restricted areas. Another example is that an organization may wish to control how many virtual machines can be spun up by employees, and, indeed, that those same machines are spun down later when they are no longer needed. So-called "rogue" cloud usage must also be detected, so that an employee setting up their own accounts for using a cloud service is detected and brought under an appropriate governance umbrella. He summarized all his findings by recommending that API keys ought to be protect in all the three delivery models because if these keys were to be stolen, then an attacker would have access to the email of every person in that organization. Protection of API Keys can be performed by encrypting them when they are stored on the file system, or by storing them within a Hardware Security Module (HSM).

Suffice to say that while O'Neill study was to highlight security concerns for cloud models service delivery models, his findings was not only shallow in content as he focused on only one security concern for every service delivery model, but also, he never touched on different security concerns that exist in the three service delivery models when deployed on either the private, public, community and hybrid clouds.

Patel (2011), employed the Cloud stack to illustrate the three different types of cloud computing service delivery models across the three main types of cloud deployment models as shown in Figure 2.3(b). He concluded that the level of abstraction is the lowest for the IaaS model where users can have higher level of control over the choice of infrastructure. On the contrary, the level of abstraction is highest for the SaaS model where users do not have much control over the platform/infrastructure. The level of control that an organization can leverage over the cloud models is lowest for the public cloud and is highest for the hybrid Cloud model. The implication here is that, SaaS users will be faced with security challenges regardless of the deployment model. The opposite is true for IaaS.

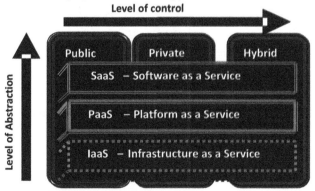

Figure 2.3(b): Cloud Stack
Source: *Patel B.D (2011)*

21

In their comparative analysis of benefits of different styles of cloud computing security, entitled *"Security Issues: Public vs Private vs Hybrid Cloud computing"*, Balasubramanian and Aramudhan (2012) reported that out of 38% of organizations that were using private cloud, 40% had serious doubts about the security of their private cloud and about 8% said that the cloud security is very weak in private cloud. The findings further revealed that public cloud services fail to meet IT and business requirements of some of the business organizations. However, they reported that hybrid cloud environment can help meet their needs because in some ways, hybrid clouds can be considered an intermediate stage as enterprises prepare to move most of their workloads to public clouds. Nevertheless, the findings shortcoming lies on the fact that not only did it dwell on security issues on three deployment models namely the private, hybrid and private and left out community cloud but also it did not mention nor rank the security concerns service delivery models vis-à-vis the aforementioned deployment models.

Kajiyama (2012), in his work on *"Cloud computing Security: How risks and threats are affecting cloud adoption decisions"*. More specifically, his research main purpose was to assess how security risk factors are affecting the existing and prospective cloud users' cloud usage strategies. His argument was that cloud adoption decisions should be made first by evaluating the current cloud service offerings, financial and technical benefits, and security concerns, and then secondly by studying real world examples that present how organizations are weighting these benefits and risks. His research findings pointed out that SaaS was the most popular type of cloud computing, with nearly 55% (54 of 95 respondents) hosting either non-critical or mission critical systems. 20% (19 of 95 respondents) indicated they were either considering or testing an SaaS implementation. IaaS and PaaS showed similar usage ratios 48 of 95 respondents nearly 50% of respondents not using, 35% either considering or testing, and 15% of them hosting either non-critical or mission-critical systems. The weakness of this study lies in the fact, the findings failed to compare which amongst cloud computing service delivery and deployment models are popular or unpopular and why considering that the four deployment models are used to host the three service models.

Nevertheless, the aforementioned previous studies in cloud computing security either dwelt only security issues of service delivery models or security concerns that emanates from use of a particular deployment model. In essence, their studies have not ventured into critical analysis of security concerns for service delivery models with their respective deployment models. It is against this backdrop that this work was studied to fill this gap of knowledge. Hence, the essence of this book was to fill this knowledge gap by presenting a different perspective of how cloud computing security

CHAPTER THREE

RESEARCH METHODOLOGY

3.1 Research Design

Kerlinger (1986) defines research design as a plan, structure or strategy of investigation so conceived as to obtain answers to research questions or problems. Comparative study research design was be employed in this study. This design was chosen because it has multi-faceted advantages such as flexibility for exploring or enhancing the "signal" (treatment) in the study. The goal was to find out why the cases are different and to reveal the general underlying structure which generates or allows such a variation. The comparative method is often used in the early stages of the development of a branch of science. It can help the researcher to ascend from the initial level of exploratory case studies to a more advanced level of general theoretical models, invariances, such as causality or evolution (Routio, 2007).

In comparative analysis, it is imperative and useful to make a factorial table, as shown in Table 3.1. This design gathered data at a particular point in time with the intention of describing the nature of the existing conditions, identifying the standards against which existing conditions can be compared and determining the relationship that exists between specific events (Kombo & Tromp, 2006). Two levels of service delivery models and four levels of deployment models were compared in a 2x4 factorial asymmetrical table.

Table 3.1: 2X4 Factorial table

		Deployment Models			
		Public	**Private**	**Community**	**Hybrid**
(Service Model)	**Secure**	r_1, r_2	r_1, r_2	r_1, r_2	r_1, r_2
	Insecure	r_1, r_2	r_1, r_2	r_1, r_2	r_1, r_2

Source: *Researcher*

Where r_1 and r_2 are replications of cloud computing security risks associated with the two selected companies.

3.2 Study Area

The study was carried out in two selected companies, both located in Nairobi, Kenya dealing with cloud computing. These two companies namely the KenyanCloud and IonaCloud were selected using purposive sampling because both have the four cloud deployment models (that is public, private, hybrid and community) and the three service delivery models(that is, SaaS, PaaS and IaaS) and therefore reflects the subject matter that the researcher intends to study and compare. The power of purposive sampling lies in selecting information which is in depth, rich and related to the central issues being studied (Kombo & Tromp, 2006). Currently, there are eight companies in Kenya actively engaged in Cloud computing services. These companies are the Safaricom, Xtranet, Quintica, Flexus technologies, PamojaCloud, IonaCloud and KenyanCloud. The companies in this sector are expected to grow tremendously owing to the availability of cheap high speed internet connectivity brought about by introduction of JTL (Jamii Telecom Limited) fibre optic cables and government futuristic policy of putting an ICT park at Konza city (Tech Mtaa, 2011)

3.3 Target Population

Target population refers to the population to be studied to which the investigator wants to generalize his results. In research, it is important that the researcher finds out as much as possible the study population. It is believed that the greater the diversity and differences that exist in the population the larger the researcher's sample size should be. Capturing the variety in population allows for more reliability of the study (Kombo & Tromp, 2006). Thus putting all these factors into consideration, the population for the study was drawn from two selected companies in Kenya dealing with cloud computing services. The study targeted two system administrators(one from each company), technicians (16 from KenyanCloud and 33 from IonaCloud) and clients (5 for KenyaCloud and 12 from Ionacloud) of the selected firms as respondents. Records in the two companies that were selected for study indicate that there were 28 and 84 employees and clients in KenyanCloud and IonaCloud respectively . Therefore the target population was 112.

3.4 Sample Size and Sampling Procedure

In order to obtain the subjects for the sample for the two selected companies, Yamane's formula for calculating the sample size was used.

$$n=N/[1+Ne^2]$$

Source: *Yamane(1967)*

where:

n= Sample size

N=Population size

E=Sampling error (usually 0.10)

The above formula was chosen because it fits in situations for comparing two groups (where analysis of variance will be the technique of analysis). Table 3.2 shows how respondents were obtained from each selected company.

Table 3.2: Sample frame

Company Name	Population size	Sample size using Yamane's Formula	Sample size		
KenyanCloud	28	22	Clients	Technicians	System administrator
			5	16	1
			KenyanCloud Subtotal Sample size		**22**
IonaCloud	84	46	Clients	Technicians	System administrator
			12	33	1
			IonaCloud Subtotal Sample size		**46**
Total Population	**112**	**Total Sample size**			**68**

Source: *Researcher*

26

The sample size for each company obtained in Table 3.2 using Yamane's formula was further divided into homogeneous subgroups (stratum) using stratified random sampling of sample sizes corresponding to groups of respondents used in the study.

While developing a sample design a researcher must pay attention to the type of universal sampling unit, size sample, parameters of interest and budgetary constraints (Kothari, 1990). An effective population must also take into consideration representation. It is important for the researcher to identify and select respondents that fulfill the questions that research is addressing. It is important that the majority of the population came from same environment. An effective population is the one that is accessible to the researcher (Kombo & Tromp, 2006). All these factors were put into consideration when the researcher was developing the sample design.

3.5 Data Collection Procedures

The researcher used a questionnaire and interview schedule to collect data from the two companies. The management of the two selected companies were notified through a letter on the intended research and also assured of confidentiality of the information obtained. Upon consent, the research instruments were then dispatched to the respondents by the researcher. Also, the researcher administered interview schedules to the systems administrators of the two companies when delivering the questionnaires to the rest of the respondents.

3.6 Pilot Study

To ensure the reliability of the questionnaire, a pilot study was carried out at Xtranet Cloud Solutions and Pamoja Cloud. These two companies were used for piloting because they had deployment and delivery models that are similar with those of KenyanCloud and IonaCloud. The instrument were revised accordingly after the pilot study, ready to be administered to the respondents in the main study.

3.7 Instrumentation

The instruments that were used to collect data are questionnaires and interview schedules. Hesse-Biber (2010) indicated that questionnaires and interviews are the most common instruments used in comparative research. The researcher chose to use

27

these instruments because the study was a comparative factorial design research. The questionnaires for all the respondents contained closed ended questions (Appendix 1 and 2). A questionnaire was chosen because it had several advantages that included not only the ability to of information being collected from a large sample size but also owing to the fact that it allowed confidentiality to be up held and saved on time of collecting data. The interview schedule for system administrators (Appendix 3) was used in the study in order to collect more information to supplement what may not have been captured by the questionnaires from the other respondents. It consisted of a written list of questions that were covered during the interview.

3.7.1 Validity of instruments

Validity concerns the extent to which the instrument measures what is intended to gauge. This means the content included in the questionnaires must be relevant to the field of study. Therefore, there was a need to determine the validity of the instrument before it is administered (Kothari, 2004).Validity is also measure of degree to which data collected using a particular instrument represented a specific domain of indicators or content of particular concept (Hesse-Biber, 2010). For this reason therefore, the developed instruments were given to the experts namely the supervisors at the Kisii university to determine validity of the instruments. The suggestions given were used to improve the instruments by identifying loopholes in time and make the necessary adjustments.

3.7.2 Reliability of instruments

Reliability is a measure of the degree of which a research instrument yields consistent results after repeated trials. Reliability ensures that there is a precision with which data is collected. If the same results are gained time after time, no matter how many times you conduct a piece of research, this suggests that the data collected is reliable (Hesse-Biber, 2010). To ensure the reliability of the questionnaires, a pilot study was carried out first before administering all the research questionnaires. This is to ensure that the items are reliable before the questionnaire are developed for the study (Aron, 1986). Reliability analysis was further determined using Cronbach's Alpha which is used as a measure of the internal consistency and reliability of an instrument. It measures how well a set of variables or items measures a single, unidimensional latent construct (Cronbach, 1951). Cronbach's Alpha is therefore not a statistical test but a coefficient of reliability or consistency. If the inter item correlations are high, then there is evidence that the items are measuring the same underlying construct. In order to ascertain this Cronbach's Alpha was computed for all the 34 items in the questionnaires for technicians and 18 items for clients . The result gave a correlation coefficient alpha value of $0.664(\approx0.7)$ and 0.770 for technicians and clients respectively (see Appendices 7 and 8 in that order). This implied that there was a strong positive correlation and reliability between the items and that there is a positive relationship and reliability between the variables used in the study.

3.8 Data Analysis and Presentation

The factorial analysis of variance was employed in comparative analysis of security concerns of the two companies. This statistical test allowed the researcher to analyse if each of the independent variables have an effect on the dependent variable (hereby called the main effects). It also allowed the researcher to determine if the main effects are independent of each other (that is, to determine if two or more independent variables interact with each other.) The data collected for the three treatments was tabulated in a format of factorial design. 2x4 Asymmetrical factorial design means two independent variables, one with 2 levels and one with 4 levels. "Condition" or "groups" is calculated by multiplying the levels, so a 2x4 design has 8 different conditions. SPSS version 19.0 was used to analyse and generate descriptive statistics and factorial ANOVA/ interaction effect charts respectively .

3.9 Ethical Considerations

All respondents involved in the study were assured of confidentiality of the information they gave. The researcher did duly informed them that information gathered during the study were to be used exclusively for academic purposes only.

CHAPTER FOUR

DATA ANALYSIS AND INTERPRETATION

4.1 Background information on technicians

The researcher was interested in finding out the background information of the technicians who participated in the study. The information covered consisted of gender, age bracket, level of education, years one has worked in Information systems environment and their exact role in the organization as indicated in Table 4.1(a). The study found out that 28(84.85%) and 7 (72.73%) respondents were male while the 5(15.15%) and 3(27.27%) were female both from IonaCloud and KenyanCloud respectively. The findings also indicated that the age brackets for all technicians involved in the two companies as respondents in the study were fairly spread with majority 18(42.42%) between age 36 to 45 years from IonaCloud and 7(63.64%) between age 18-24 at KenyanCloud. From age 25 to 35 was found to be another common group of technicians who constituted 11(33.33%) from IonaCloud and 2(18.18%) from KenyanCloud.

The background results also revealed that whereas majority 17(51.52%) of respondents at IonaCloud were degree holders, the opposite was true at IonaCloud where majority 6(54.55%) were tertiary certificate holders. Respondents were also asked to indicate the length of duration they have been working in the field of Information technology/systems. As evidenced in Table 4.1 (a), the results showed that majority 17(51.52%) at IonaCloud have been in this field for over 5 years which implies that they had enough experience in matters of information systems and emerging trends like cloud computing. On the contrary, the results further revealed that at KenyanCloud, majority 5(45.45%) of responds have worked below one year while the rest were 3(27.27%) apiece.

30

Table 4.1(a): Comparison of Summary background information of the Technicians at IonaCloud and KenyanCloud

	IonaCloud		KenyanCloud	
Gender of Respondents				
Item	**Frequency**	**Percent**	**Frequency**	**Percent**
Male	28	84.85	8	72.73
Female	5	15.15	3	27.27
TOTAL	**33**	**100.0**	**11**	**100.0**
Age bracket				
Item	**Frequency**	**Percent**	**Frequency**	**Percent**
18-24	8	24.24	7	63.64
25-35	11	33.33	2	18.18
36-45	14	42.42	2	18.18
Total	**33**	**100.0**	**11**	**100.0**
Level of qualification				
Tertiary	16	48.49	6	54.55
Degree	17	51.51	5	45.45
Total	**33**	**100.0**	**11**	**100.0**
Years worked in information systems				
Below 1 year	8	24.24	**5**	45.45
1-2 years	8	24.24	3	27.27
Over 5 years	17	51.52	3	27.27
Total	**33**	**100.0**	**11**	**100.0**

Source: *Researcher*

While still focusing on backround information of the respondents from the two companies, the researcher further sought to interrogate the specific roles the technicians they do on a daily basis. When respondents at IonaCloud were asked to indicate their exact role in the company, majority 27(81.82%) of respondents were technicians as depicted in Figure 4.1(a) while 4(12.12%) dealt directly with security or administrative matters of the information system. The rest 2(6.06%) played other information systems related roles in the company.

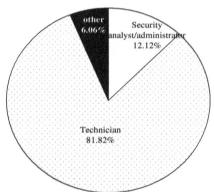

Figure 4.1(a) Technicians role at IonaCloud
Source: *Researcher*

In KenyanCloud, results also showed that majority 6(54.55%) of respondents were technicians as depicted in Figure 4.1(b) whereas 3(27.27%) belonged to the docket of security or administrative in the information system department of the company . Unlike in IonaCloud, the remainder 2(18.18%) of respondents did other roles in the related to Information systems in the company.

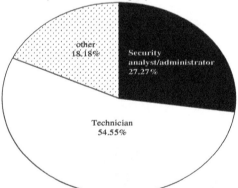

Figure 4.1(b) Technicians role at KenyanCloud
Source: *Researcher*

32

Table 4.1(b): Comparison of Percentage Proportion of years one has worked in the company.

Length of time	IonaCloud		KenyanCloud	
	Frequency	Percent	Frequency	Percent
Less than a year	10	30.30	4	36.36
Less than two years	12	36.36	6	54.55
Less than three years	6	18.18	1	9.09
Less than four years	5	15.15	0	0.00
Total	33	100.0	11	100.0

Source: *Researcher*

Respondents were asked to indicate the length of time they have been working in the current organization. The essence of this question is that the researcher was interested to know how familiar the respondents were with current organization's computing structures. From Table 4.1 (b), the findings in the two companies had similar pattern where majority 12(36.36%) at IonaCloud and 6(54.55%) at KenyanCloud had worked for less than two years, while 10(30.30%) and 4(36.36%) had company working experience of less than one year respectively. A paltry of 5(15.15%) in IonaCloud had a company working experience of less than four years but no such respondents for KenyanCloud, perhaps due the fact that the company is still new in the market .

4.2 Service delivery model with their respective deployment models

Respondents in the study were presented with a list of possible cloud computing security issues .The respondents were asked to "strongly agree" "agree" "Disagree" "strongly disagree" They were also asked to indicate whether they were "undecided" incase they were not sure. The questions revolved around cloud computing security concerns in three delivery models namely the SaaS, PaaS and IaaS with respective with the kind of deployment models (public, private, community and hybrid) used to deliver the aforementioned delivery services. The bi-polar adjectives were collapsed into "agree", "disagree" and "undecided". Data for "strongly disagree" and "disagree" were amalgamated together. Data on "undecided" was not interfered with. Subsequent tables below shows the comparative data findings for the two companies under study namely the IonaCloud and KenyanCloud.

Table 4.2(a): Comparative analysis of SaaS delivery model with their respective deployment models at IonaCloud and KenyanCloud

Variable	Company	Agree	Undecided	Disagree	Total
Data/information in transit while using SaaS delivery model are always safe regardless of the deployment model used	IonaCloud	9 (27.27%)	1 (3.03%)	23 (69.70%)	33 (100.0%)
	KenyanCloud	1 (9.09%)	1 (9.09%)	9 (81.82%)	11 (100.0%)
In SaaS delivery model, some deployment models allows unauthorized access to data/information in your cloud	IonaCloud	16 (38.6%)	0 (0.00%)	17 (59.1%)	33 (100.0%)
	KenyanCloud	3 (27.27%)	2 (18.18%)	6 (54.55%)	11 (100.0%)
In SaaS delivery model, data deployed on private cloud is safe	IonaCloud	24 (72.73%)	0 (0.00%)	9 (27.27%)	33 (100.0%)
	KenyanCloud	6 (54.55%)	2 (18.18%)	3 (27.27%)	11 (100.0%)
In SaaS delivery model, data deployed on public cloud is safe	IonaCloud	7 (21.21%)	2 (6.06%)	24 (72.72%)	33 (100.0%)
	KenyanCloud	2 (18.18%)	4 (36.36%)	5 (45.46%)	11 (100.0%)
In SaaS delivery model, data deployed on community cloud is safe	IonaCloud	9 (27.27%)	6 (18.18%)	18 (54.55%)	33 (100.0%)
	KenyanCloud	3 (27.27%)	2 (18.18%)	6 (54.55%)	11 (100.0%)
In SaaS delivery model, data deployed on hybrid cloud is safe	IonaCloud	18 (54.55%)	8 (24.24%)	7 (21.21%)	33 (100.0%)
	KenyanCloud	5 (45.46%)	4 (36.36%)	2 (18.18%)	11 (100.0%)
SaaS are vulnerable for improper access control, virtual machines operating systems flaws, cookies and hidden field manipulation as well as insecure storages and configurations	IonaCloud	0 (0.00%)	16 (48.48%)	17 (51.52%)	33 (100.0%)
	KenyanCloud	4 (36.36%)	4 (36.36%)	3 (27.27%)	11 (100.0%)
In SaaS model, hackers can manipulate weakness in data security model to get an illegitimate access to data or application	IonaCloud	0 (0.00%)	8 (24.24%)	25 (7.76%)	33 (100.0%)
	KenyanCloud	0 (0.00%)	3 (27.27%)	8 (72.73%)	11 (100.0%)

Source: *Researcher*

Respondents were asked to indicate whether they agreed or disagreed with various SaaS delivery model cloud computing related security concerns. From Table 4.2(a), the respondents showed that majority 23(69.70%) from IonaCloud and 9(81.82%) from KenyanCloud disagreed to the fact that data or information on transit always safe regardless of the deployment model employed. Nevertheless, a striking results

34

showed that almost a third 9(27.27%) of respondents from IonaCloud which was quite a contrast of respondents from KenyanCloud 1(9.09%) who both agreed that data or information are always safe while on transit using SaaS delivery model. Only 1(3.03%) and 1(9.09%) were undecided from IonaCloud and KenyanCloud in that order. When asked as to whether, some deployment models allows unauthorized access to data/information in their cloud in SaaS delivery model, respondents from IonaCloud equidistantly responded where 17(51.52%) disagreed while 16(48.49%) agreed, the opposite was true for KenyanCloud where a overwhelming 9(81.82%) disagreed.

Nevertheless, respondents were fronted with pertinent questions to give their reactions as to whether SaaS services delivered on various cloud deployment models namely the private, public, community and hybrid clouds are all safe. As one would easily guess, majority 24(72.73%) of respondents from IonaCloud and 6(54.55%) of respondents from KenyanCloud agreed that SaaS services delivered on private cloud are always safe against 9(27.27%) and 3(27.27%) who equally disagreed in the same proportion that private cloud is not always a safe cloud model to deploy SaaS services in the two companies in that order. As to whether deploying SaaS services in public cloud was safe, 24(72.72%) respondents IonaCloud strongly disagreed while 5(45.46%) respondents from KenyanCloud mildly disagreed. Infact, 4(36.36%) of respondents from KenyanCloud were undecided. Also, the findings in Table 4.2(a) revealed that equal number of respondents at 18(54.55%) from IonaCloud and 6(54.55%) from KenyanCloud disagreed to the fact SaaS data deployed on community cloud is safe; similarly, identical results were further exhibited by respondents with 6(18.18%) from IonaCloud and 2(18.18%) from KenyanCloud undecided. Equally significant results showed that most 18(54.55%) from IonaCloud and 5(45.46%) from KenyanCloud respondents agreed that hybrid cloud is safe to deploy SaaS services while 7(21.21%) and 2(18.18%) from the respective companies disagreed.

Summative questions were posed to respondents to give their feelings as to whether SaaS is vulnerable for improper access control, virtual machines operating systems flaws, cookies and hidden field manipulation as well as insecure storages and configurations as well as to the fact that hackers can manipulate weakness in data

35

security model to get an illegitimate access to data or application. At IonaCloud, 17 (51.52%) agreed and the rest 16(48.48%) were undecided, the opposite results from KenyanCloud were reported with 4(36.36%) agreeing and equally undecided in equal measure when they were asked whether SaaS delivery model is vulnerable due to improper access control or VMs operating system flaws and similar weaknesses. Finally, as to whether hackers can manipulate weaknesses in SaaS model to get illegitimate access to data/information, most 25(75.76%) of respondents from IonaCloud strongly disagreed while 8(24.24%) were undecided, and similar results of respondents from KenyanCloud with 8(72.73%) disagreeing and 3(27.27%) being undecided.

Table 4.2(b): Comparative analysis of PaaS delivery model with their respective deployment models IonaCloud and KenyanCloud companies

Statement	Company	A	U	D	Total
Your company lack interoperability and integration that pose a security risk and challenges to PaaS model	IonaCloud	31 (93.94%)	1 (3.03%)	1 (3.03%)	33 (100.0%)
	KenyanCloud	0 (0.00%)	0 (0.00%)	11 (100.00%)	11 (100.0%)
There is lack of secure software development process with PaaS platform	IonaCloud	8 (24.24%)	0 (0.00%)	25 (75.76%)	33 (100.0%)
	KenyanCloud	4 (36.36%)	0 (0.00%)	7 (63.63%)	11 (100.0%)
In PaaS, there is a vendor Lock-In problem due to migration problems	IonaCloud	6 (18.18%)	8 (24.24%)	19 (57.56%)	33 (100.0%)
	KenyanCloud	1 (9.09%)	3 (27.27%)	7 (63.63%)	11 (100.0%)
PaaS service model is built on Service Oriented architecture (SOA) model which inherits security issues that exists in SOA model	IonaCloud	14 (42.42%)	0 (0.00%)	19 (57.56%)	33 (100.0%)
	KenyanCloud	4 (36.36%)	0 (0.00%)	7 (63.63%)	11 (100.0%)
Applications created with much different type of Application Programming Interface (APIs) could create potential security threat due to incompatibility and integration issues	IonaCloud	33 (100.00%)	0 (0.00%)	0 (0.00%)	33 (100.0%)
	KenyanCloud	11 (100.00%)	0 (0.00%)	0 (0.00%)	11 (100.0%)
In PaaS delivery model, data deployed on private cloud is safe	IonaCloud	29 (87.87%)	3 (9.09%)	1 (3.03%)	33 (100.0%)
	KenyanCloud	7 (63.63%)	2 (18.18%)	2 (18.18%)	11 (100.0%)
In PaaS delivery model, data deployed on public cloud is safe	IonaCloud	10 (30.30%)	0 (0.00%)	23 (69.70%)	33 (100.0%)
	KenyanCloud	2 (18.18%)	0 (0.00%)	9 (81.82%)	11 (100.0%)

In PaaS delivery model, data deployed on community cloud is safe	IonaCloud	6 (18.18%)	2 (6.06%)	25 (75.76%)	33 (100.0%)
	KenyanCloud	7 (63.63%)	2 (18.18%)	2 (18.18%)	11 (100.0%)
In PaaS delivery model, data deployed on hybrid cloud is safe	IonaCloud	27 (81.82%)	0 (0.00%)	6 (18.18%)	33 (100.0%)
	KenyanCloud	4 (36.36%)	1 (9.09%)	6 (54.55%)	11 (100.0%)

Source:*Researcher*

In order to understand how PaaS service delivery model and its deployment models works, various questions were posed to the respondents to give their feelings. One of such salient questions was as to whether the company lacked interoperability and integration that could pose a security risk and challenges to PaaS model. A staggering 31(93.94%) and 11(100.00%) of respondents from IonaCloud and KenyanCloud respectively vehemently disagreed to it. Respondents were asked to agree or disagree to the fact that there is lack of secure software development process with PaaS platform. In Table 4.2(c) the findings clearly shows that 25(75.76%) of respondents from IonaCloud and 7(63.63%) of respondents from KenyanCloud disagreed with almost equal proportion of respondents 8(24.24%) and 4(36.36%) consenting to the PaaS security concern as being a weakness in the two companies.

Respondents were further asked as to whether in PaaS model, they usually face a vendor Lock-In problem due to migration problems. From IonaCloud, 19(57.56%) respondents disagreed while6(18.18%) agreeing that indeed such migratory related problems exist in PaaS platform, although a fairly good number of respondents 8(24.24%) were undecided. Likewise, respondents from KenyanCloud exhibited similar patterns with their counterparts in IonaCloud, with 7(63.63%) disagreeing to the existence of vendor lock-in problems while 3(27.27%) were hesitantly undecided. This may be attributed to the fact that various cloud providers use a PaaS platform that is portable across different vendors' platforms.

As evidenced in Table 4.2 (b), 19(57.56%) of the respondents from IonaCloud and 7(63.63%) were of the contrary opinion that that PaaS service model are built on Service Oriented architecture (SOA) model they inherits security issues that exists in SOA model. However, almost equal percentage of respondents from the two companies concur that SOA inherited issues such as DoS attacks, MITM, XML

37

related attacks, dictionary attacks, replay attacks, SQL injection attacks and data entry validation related attacks being rampant threats in PaaS delivery model. A related question to the SOA model PaaS problem was also fronted to the respondents as to whether applications created with much different type of Application Programming Interface (APIs) creates potential security threat due to incompatibility and integration issues in the cloud. Interestingly, all respondents 33(100.00%) from IonaCloud and 11(100.00%) from KenyanCloud unanimously agreed.

Moreover, the respondents were asked to give their feelings as to whether PaaS services delivered on various cloud deployment models namely the private, public, community and hybrid clouds are all safe. The findings in Table 4.2 (b) shows that 29(87.87%) of respondents from IonaCloud and 7(63.63%) from KenyanCloud are of the agreement that PaaS services deployed on private cloud are always safe although a fair portion 2(18.18%) of the respondents from KenyanCloud were not sure of the safety of this deployment model. Only 10(30.30%) and 2(18.18%) of respondents from IonaCloud and KenyanCloud respectively agreed that PaaS services hosted on public cloud are safe but majority 23(69.70%) from IonaCloud and 9(81.82%) disagreed. Quite contrasting results were exhibited in respondents feelings towards PaaS being deployed in community cloud. Results indicated that whereas majority 25(75.76%) of respondents from IonaCloud disagreed, there was a sharp contrast in response from KenyanCloud with 7(63.63%) assenting that community cloud is safe for deploying and delivering PaaS services. Results worth mentioning is that majority 27(81.82%) and 5(54.55%) of respondents from IonaCloud and KenyanCloud correspondingly agreed that hybrid cloud is a safe platform for hosting and deploying PaaS services.

Table 4.2 (c) shows the findings of respondents feelings regarding various issues related to IaaS services when hosted in different deployment models in the cloud.
The researcher was interested to know from the respondents technical point of view the security of virtual machines (VM) boundaries that in the event that the company misconfigures or mismanage whether it could lead to unauthorized access and data leaks regardless of deployment model used. As can be seen in Table 4.2(c), Majority 23(69.70%) and 6(54.55%) of respondents from IonaCloud and KenyanCloud respectively agreed while 10(30.30%) and 5(45.45%) disagreed. A closely related VM issues such as memory leaks, VM images attacks from malicious injection codes,

risk of re-using VM templates and hypervisor weaknesses were also posed again to get the respondents feelings from the technical know-how point of view. The results indicated that majority 18(54.55%) and 7(63.64%) of respondents from IonaCloud and KenyanCloud in that order, disagreed that malware, DOS and memory leaks are most common threats regardless of deployment used in IaaS services whereas 14(42.42%) and 2(18.18%) of the respondents from two aforementioned companies were in agreement.

Table 4.2(c): Comparative analysis of IaaS delivery model with their respective deployment models in IonaCloud and KenyanCloud companies.

Statement	Company	A	U	D	Total
In IaaS, securing VM boundaries is your responsibility but misconfiguration or mismanagement could lead to unauthorized access and data leaks regardless of deployment model used	IonaCloud	23 (69.70%)	0 (0.00%)	10 (30.30%)	33 (100.0%)
	KenyanCloud	6 (54.55%)	0 (0.00%)	5 (45.45%)	11 (100.0%)
In IaaS, malware, DOS, memory leaks and other VM operating system are most common threats regardless of deployment used	IonaCloud	14 (42.42%)	1 (3.03%)	18 (54.55%)	33 (100.0%)
	KenyanCloud	2 (18.18%)	2 (18.18%)	7 (63.64%)	11 (100.0%)
VMs images are under the risk of malicious codes injection when offline and these VM files can be stolen to	IonaCloud	22 (66.67%)	4 (12.12%)	7 (21.21%)	33 (100.0%)
	KenyanCloud	8 (72.73%)	1 (9.09%)	2 (18.18%)	11 (100.0%)
VM templates can be used as rapid deployment system and all these templates may contain the original owner information which may be re-used for new customers	IonaCloud	18 (54.55%)	0 (0.00%)	15 (45.45%)	33 (100.0%)
	KenyanCloud	8 (72.73%)	0 (0.00%)	3 (27.27%)	11 (100.0%)
In IaaS model, since we provide the security of hypevisor, any vulnerability in hypervisor software inherits security risks in customer VMs	IonaCloud	0 (0.00%)	2 (6.06%)	31 (93.94%)	33 (100.0%)
	KenyanCloud	0 (0.00%)	0 (0.00%)	11 (100.0%)	11 (100.0%)
Storage of data/Information and applications locations in IaaS delivery model are always safe regardless of the deployment model used	IonaCloud	24 (72.73%)	0 (0.00%)	9 (27.27%)	33 (100.0%)
	KenyanCloud	3 (27.27%)	2 (18.18%)	6 (54.55%)	11 (100.0%)
In IaaS delivery model, data deployed on private cloud is safe	IonaCloud	31 (93.94%)	1 (3.03%)	1 (3.03%)	33 (100.0%)

	KenyanCloud	8 (72.73%)	2 (18.18%)	1 (9.09%)	11 (100.0%)
In IaaS delivery model, data deployed on public cloud is safe	IonaCloud	3 (9.09%)	4 (12.12%)	26 (78.79%)	33 (100.0%)
	KenyanCloud	2 (18.18%)	1 (9.09%)	8 (72.73%)	11 (100.0%)
In IaaS delivery model, data deployed on community cloud is safe	IonaCloud	6 (18.18%)	8 (24.24%)	19 (57.58%)	33 (100.0%)
	KenyanCloud	2 (18.18%)	3 (27.27%)	6 (54.55%)	11 (100.0%)
In IaaS delivery model, data deployed on hybrid cloud is safe	IonaCloud	13 (39.39%)	8 (24.24%)	12 (36.36%)	33 (100.0%)
	KenyanCloud	7 (63.64%)	2 (18.18%)	2 (18.18%)	11 (100.0%)

Source: *Researcher*

On the contrary, most respondents 22(66.67%) from IonaCloud and 8(72.73%) from KenyanCloud agreed that when VM templates are used as rapid deployment system, they may contain the original owner information might be re-used for new customers hence posing a security risk in IaaS platform. However, almost all respondents 31(93.94%) from IonaCloud and 11(100.00%) from KenyanCloud disagreed to the fact that any vulnerability in hypervisor software usually inherits security risks in customer VMs. It was also revealed that while majority 24(72.73%) of respondents from IonaCloud agreed that storage of data/Information and applications locations in IaaS delivery model are always safe regardless of the deployment model used, majority 6(54.55%) of their counterparts at KenyanCloud of were of the contrary opinion.

When respondents were asked to indicate which cloud deployment model was safest for delivering IaaS services, 31(93.94%) of IonaCloud respondents and 8(72.73%) of KenyanCloud respondents understandably agreed that private cloud is safe, with almost a fifth 2(18.18%) of KenyanCloud respondents being of the contrary opinion. Public cloud and community were almost similarly rated by respondents as being highly vulnerable to cloud security threats and not fit for delivering IaaS services. Up to 26(78.79%) and 8(72.73%) as well as 19(57.58%) and 6(54.55%) that both the public and community deployment models respectively disagreed that they are not safe in both IonaCloud and KenyanCloud companies correspondingly, although a considerable number of respondents were not sure about the safety of these two aforementioned deployment models. However, a substantial number 7(63.64%) of respondents at KenyanCloud supported the idea that hybrid cloud was a Safe cloud to deploy IaaS services but not for respondents from IonaCloud who registered a paltry of 13(39.39%) also concurring with safety of the hybrid cloud being a better option to deploy IaaS services.

4.3 Background information of clients

Furthermore, the researcher also sought to interrogate the background information of the clients who participated in the study from IonaCloud and KenyanCloud companies. Just like the technicians respondents, the information covered also consisted of gender, age bracket and highest level of education one had attained. Table 4.3(a), shows the analysis results. The findings shows that there was an almost equal gender disparity in the two companies with IonaCloud having 7(77.8%) male respondents versus 3(75.00%) male respondents from KenyanCloud. The rest, 2(22.22%) and 1(15.00) were female respondents from the companies respectively. The findings also indicated that the age brackets for all clients used as respondents in the study were fairly spread with majority 7(77.78%) from IonaCloud and 4(100.00%) from KenyanCloud whose age bracket were between 25 to 35 years.

Table 4.3(a): Background information of clients

	IonaCloud		KenyanCloud	
Gender of Respondents (Clients)				
Item	**Frequency**	**Percent**	**Frequency**	**Percent**
Male	7	77.78	3	75.00
Female	2	22.22	1	15.00
TOTAL	**9**	**100.0**	**4**	**100.0**
Age bracket				
	IonaCloud		**KenyanCloud**	
25-35	7	77.78	4	100.00
36-45	2	22.22	0	0.00
Total	**9**	**100.0**		**100.0**
Level of qualification				
	IonaCloud		**KenyanCloud**	
Tertiary	3	33.33	1	15.00
Degree	5	55.56	3	75.00
Masters	1	11.11	0	0.00
Total	**9**	**100.0**		**100.0**

Source: *Researcher.*

Over half of the total number of clients used as respondents in the study from the two companies indicated that majority have at least a degree certificate with 3(75.0%) from KenyanCloud and 5(55.56%) from IonaCloud. This implies that the clients of the two aforementioned companies are knowledgeable as far as level of education is concerned and can make a sound judgment when choosing the services from the cloud and putting various security concerns in question.

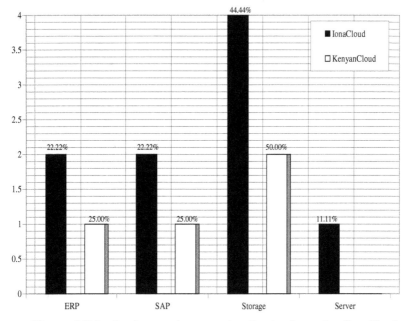

Figure 4.3(a): Services customers subscribe to from the IonaCloud and KenyanCloud cloud computing service providers
Source: *Researcher*

Figure 4.3 (a) depicts the type of services clients subscribe from the cloud computing providers companies namely the IonaCloud and KenyanCloud. As it can be seen, 2(50.00%) of the respondents (clients) from KenyanCloud and 4(44.44%) of the respondents from IonaCloud mostly subscribed to storage media services from IaaS platform, with similar proportion of clients 1(25.00%) from KenyanCloud and 2(22.22%) from IonaCloud having equal subscription rate to enterprise resource planning(ERP) software and SAP software(which can be integrated with ERP). Subscription to cloud server was the least popular 1(11.11%) services requested by clients from IonaCloud. KenyanCloud clients did not subscribe to server IaaS services from their cloud computing service providers.

Table 4.3(b): Comparison analysis of Clients response on SaaS delivery model with their respective deployment models in IonaCloud and KenyanCloud

Variable	Company	Agree	Undecided	Disagree	Total
In SaaS delivery model, data deployed on private cloud is safe	IonaCloud	8 (88.89%)	0 (0.00%)	1 (11.11%)	9 (100.0%)
	KenyanCloud	3 (75.00%)	0 (0.00%)	1 (25.00%)	4 (100.0%)
In SaaS delivery model, data deployed on public cloud is safe	IonaCloud	2 (22.22%)	2 (22.22%)	5 (55.56%)	9 (100.0%)
	KenyanCloud	1 (25.00%)	0 (0.00%)	3 (75.00%)	4 (100.0%)
In SaaS delivery model, data deployed on community cloud is safe	IonaCloud	1 (11.11%)	1 (11.11%)	7 (77.78%)	9 (100.0%)
	KenyanCloud	1 (25.00%)	1 (25.00%)	2 (50.00%)	4 (100.0%)
In SaaS delivery model, data deployed on hybrid cloud is safe	IonaCloud	5 (55.56%)	2 (22.22%)	2 (22.22%)	9 (100.0%)
	KenyanCloud	2 (50.00%)	1 (25.00%)	1 (25.00%)	4 (100.0%)

Source: *Researcher*

As a way of obtaining replication of data from respondents which was later used in factorial design and analysis, similar but simple questions given to technicians were also issued to clients from the two companies under study.

The findings from Table 4.3(b) indicates that the clients feelings are in agreement to that of technicians with majority 8(88.89%) from IonaCloud and 3(75.00%) from KenyanCloud, agreeing that private clouds are safest models to deploy and deliver SaaS services. Moreover, same resonance was exhibited by 5(55.56%) and 2(50.00%) clients from IonaCloud and KenyanCloud respectively ascribing to the fact that hybrid cloud is a safe deployment model to host SaaS services in the cloud. However, a considerable equal number of clients were both undecided as well as disagreeing on the safeness of hybrid cloud. Nevertheless, 7(77.78%) of clients from IonaCloud and 2(50.00%) clients from KenyanCloud were had low opinion on the safeness of both public and community deployment clouds as models of deployment SaaS services in the cloud.

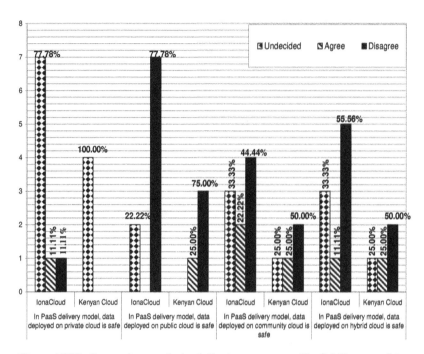

Figure 4.3(b): Comparison analysis of clients responses on PaaS delivery model with their respective deployment models at IonaCloud and KenyanCloud
Source: *Researcher*

The results in Figure 4.3(b) shows that, just in SaaS delivery model, the most preferred cloud for deploying PaaS services by clients are private 7(77.78%) and 4(100.0%) for Ionacloud and KenyanCloud respectively. However, as opposed to SaaS model, 2(50.00%) of the KenyanCloud clients and 5(55.56%) of IonaCloud clients had low opinion on the safety of hybrid cloud when used to deploy PaaS services on the cloud. A similar and more resounding pattern for the least popular clouds in terms of safety was also found to be public cloud 7(77.78%) and 3(75.00%) by IonaCloud and KenyanCloud clients respectively. In addition, IonaCloud and KenyanCloud customers mildly agreed at 3(33.33%) and 2(25.00%) correspondingly that community cloud could be the safest model for deploying PaaS services on the cloud.

45

Table 4.3(c): Comparative analysis of clients responses on IaaS delivery model with their respective deployment models at IonaCloud and KenyanCloud

Variable question	Company	Agree	Undecided	Disagree	Total
In IaaS delivery model, data deployed on private cloud is safe	IonaCloud	8 (88.89%)	0 (0.00%)	1 (11.11%)	9 (100.0%)
	KenyanCloud	3 (75.00%)	0 (0.00%)	1 (25.00%)	4 (100.0%)
In IaaS delivery model, data deployed on public cloud is safe	IonaCloud	1 (11.11%)	1 (11.11%)	7 (77.78%)	9 (100.0%)
	KenyanCloud	0 (0.00%)	1 (25.00%)	3 (75.00%	4 (100.0%)
In IaaS delivery model, data deployed on community cloud is safe	IonaCloud	1 (11.11%)	2 (22.22%)	6 (66.67%)	9 (100.0%)
	KenyanCloud	2(50.00%)	0(0.00%)	2(50.00%)	4(100.0%)
In IaaS delivery model, data deployed on hybrid cloud is safe	IonaCloud	6 (66.67%)	1 (11.11%)	2 (22.22%)	9 (100.0%)
	KenyanCloud	2 (50.00%)	0 (0.00%)	2 (50.00%)	4 (100.0%)

Source: *Researcher*

As exhibited in the aforementioned delivery models namely SaaS and PaaS, similar results were also demonstrated in Table 4.3(c) by clients showing their preference to the private cloud with 8(88.89%) from IonaCloud and 3(75.00%) from KenyanCloud who attested it is the safest model for deploying IaaS services. Likewise, there was very low opinion on safeness of public cloud with 7(77.78%) from IonaCloud and 3(75.00%) from KenyanCloud disagreeing to its safety. Interestingly, whereas 2(50.00%) of clients from KenyanCloud agreed that community cloud was safe to deploy IaaS services in the cloud, their counterparts 1(11.11%) in IonaCloud only agreed. Last but not least, Table 4.3(c) also shows very important results as far as hybrid cloud safety is concerned. Upto 6(66.67%) number of clients from IonaCloud agreed that hybrid cloud is secure to deploy IaaS services against 2(22.22%) who though it be insecure. However, KenyanCloud clients equally agreed and disagreed 2(50.00%) apiece that hybrid cloud is safe and at the same time vulnerable to cloud computing security risks.

Table 4.3(d): Comparative analysis of Clients responses on lack of cloud control or autonomy in IonaCloud and KenyanCloud

Variable question	Company	Yes	No	Total
Cloud computing supplier maintains security monitoring logs of all access to your data and documents as routine, random, audit or suspicious leveraging their prescribed scripts and operational procedures as the basis for all audit in all deployment models	IonaCloud	5 (55.56%)	4 (44.44%)	9 (100.0%)
	KenyanCloud	2 (50.00%)	2 (50.00%	4 (100.0%)
User access control rules, security policies and enforcement are managed by the cloud provider irrespective of the deployment model used	IonaCloud	4 (44.44%)	5 (55.56%)	9 (100.0%)
	KenyanCloud	2 (50.00%	2 (50.00%	4 (100.0%)
In SaaS, applications are multi-tenant hosted by 3rd party usually exposes functionality via XML based APIs.	IonaCloud	3 (33.33%)	6 (66.67%)	9 (100.0%)
	KenyanCloud	1 (25.00%)	3 (75.00%)	4 (100.0%)

Source: *Researcher*

Finally, clients were asked to respond to cloud control related questions and as tabulated in Table 4.3(d), the findings   shows that 5(55.56%) and 2(50.00%) of clients from IonaCloud and KenyanCloud respectively, averagely approved the fact that   Cloud computing suppliers should maintain security monitoring logs of all access to their data and documents as the basis for audit in all deployment models, but had their own reservations for disapproving such control measure. However, 2(50.00%) of respondents from KenyanCloud did not like the idea of leaving monitoring logs to their cloud computing service providers irrespective of the type of deployment model used. In addition, 5(55.56%) and 2(50.00%) of the respondents weakly rejected the idea   that their access control rules, security policies and enforcement should be   managed by the cloud computing service providers irrespective of the deployment model used. Lastly, respondents were asked to give their opinion as to whether SaaS applications that are multi-tenant and hosted by third party exposes functionality via XML based APIs. Majority 6(66.67%) and 3(75.00%) of respondents from IonaCloud and KenyanCloud respectively strongly disagreed while 3(33.33%) and 1(25.00%) concurred affirmatively in that order.

4.4 Factorial design Analysis.

Besides using descriptive statistics, the researcher was interested to ascertain whether there exists an interaction or main effects between the variables used in this study.

Thus the factorial analysis of variance (ANOVA) was employed in this section. This design is an inferential statistic which allowed the researcher to test if each of the independent variables have an effect on the dependent variable (hereby called the main effects). It also allowed the researcher to determine if the main effects are independent of each other (That is, to determine if two or more independent variables interact with each other.)

The data collected were coded and computed from the proportion of those who agreed and disagreed and tabulated in 2x4 factorial design format (See appendices 4 and 5 for tabulated results for technicians and clients respectively). In the subsequent sections, the data obtained from cloud deployment models were computed and run against data obtained from delivery models using a factorial ANOVA and interaction graphs.

4.5 SaaS delivery model versus cloud deployment models

Data obtained from descriptive statistics results were recorded appropriately in SPSS version 19.0 and factorial analysis computed. The results generated are Factorial ANOVA table which contains F-value used to reject or accept the null hypothesis based on 5% level of significance and a factorial design graph to check if there is any interaction effect between levels of main factors.

Table 4.5(a): Between-Subjects factors SaaS levels

Between-Subjects Factors			
		Value Label	N
Deployment model used	1	Private	4
	2	Public	4
	3	Community	4
	4	Hybrid	4
SaaS Security Status	1	Secure SaaS	8
	2	Insecure SaaS	8

Source:*Researcher*

48

The Between-Subject Factors that appear in Table 4.5(a) provide information regarding the categories involved in the analysis.

Table 4.5 (b): ANOVA of SaaS delivery model versus deployment model used

Tests of Between-Subjects Effects					
Dependent Variable:Replication					
Source	Type III Sum of Squares	df	Mean Square	F	Sig.
Corrected Model	665.750[a]	7	95.107	2.174	.149
Intercept	1980.250	1	1980.250	45.263	.000
SaaS_Status	1.000	1	1.000	.023	.884
DeploymentModel	78.750	3	26.250	.600	.633
SaaS_Status * DeploymentModel	586.000	3	195.333	4.465	.040
Error	350.000	8	43.750		
Total	2996.000	16			
Corrected Total	1015.750	15			
a. R Squared = .655 (Adjusted R Squared = .354)					

Source:*Researcher*

The findings from Table 4.5(b) indicates that the interaction effect (that is, deployment model * SaaS status) has a significant difference with results of (F=4.465, p = .040). However, the results for both the main effects namely deployment model(F=0.023, p =.884) and SaaS status(F=.006, p = .633) are were not statistically significant.

In addition, if we examine Figure 4.5(a), we can visualize a high interaction effect between factors (SaaS delivery model and deployment models). The figure clearly depicts that SaaS services deployed on community cloud are highly insecure. Interestingly, the results indicates that private, public and hybrid clouds are equally secure models for deploying SaaS services.

Since the P-values for main interaction effects between deployment models and SaaS security status effects are (F=4.465, p = .040<0.05), the null hypothesis (H0)) was rejected and conclusion was reached that that SaaS service delivery model and their respective deployment models used have significant effect on cloud computing security in the selected firms in Kenya. Hence the SaaS delivery model is dependent on the type of deployment model used to host and deliver its services in the cloud.

Estimated Marginal Means of Replication

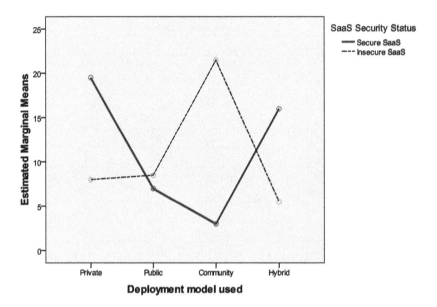

Figure 4.5(a): A graph depicting interaction effect between SaaS delivery model and deployment models
Source:*Researcher*

4.7 PaaS delivery model versus cloud deployment models

In a similar pattern with SaaS, data obtained from descriptive statistics results from PaaS were recorded appropriately in SPSS version 19.0 and factorial analysis computed. The results generated are Factorial ANOVA table which contains F-value used to reject or accept null hypothesis based on 5% level of significance and factorial graph to check if there is any interaction effect between levels of main factors.

Table 4.6(a): Between-Subjects factors PaaS levels

Between-Subjects Factors			
		Value Label	N
PaaS Security Status	1	Secure PaaS	8
	2	Insecure PaaS	8
Deployment model used	1	Private	4
	2	Public	4
	3	Community	4
	4	Hybrid	4

Source:*Researcher*

Table 4.6(b): ANOVA of PaaS delivery model versus deployment model used

Tests of Between-Subjects Effects					
Dependent Variable:Replication					
Source	Type III Sum of Squares	df	Mean Square	F	Sig.
Corrected Model	1222.438[a]	7	174.634	1.942	.186
Intercept	2943.062	1	2943.062	32.723	.000
PaaS_Status	.563	1	.563	.006	.939
DeploymentModel	16.188	3	5.396	.060	.979
PaaS_Status * DeploymentModel	1205.688	3	401.896	4.469	.040
Error	719.500	8	89.938		
Total	4885.000	16			
Corrected Total	1941.938	15			
a. R Squared = .629 (Adjusted R Squared = .305)					

Source: *Researcher*

The findings from Table 4.6 (b) above indicates that the interaction significant difference between the main effects(deployment model * PaaS status) with results (F=4.469, p = .040), while the results for both the deployment model(, F=.006, p =.939) and PaaS status(F=.060, p = .979) are not statistically significant.

In addition, if we examine Figure 4.6(a) below, we can visualize a high interaction effect between of main factors (PaaS delivery model and deployment models). The graph clearly depicts that PaaS services deployed on community and public clouds are highly insecure. On the other hand, the graph visually indicates that hybrid cloud is highly secure model for deploying PaaS services than private cloud, although both are considerably secure clouds.

Since the P-values for main interaction effects between deployment models and SaaS security status effects are (F=4.4469, p = .040<0.05), we reject H_0 and conclude that PaaS service delivery model and the respective deployment models used have significant effect on cloud computing security in the selected firms in Kenya.

Estimated Marginal Means of Replication

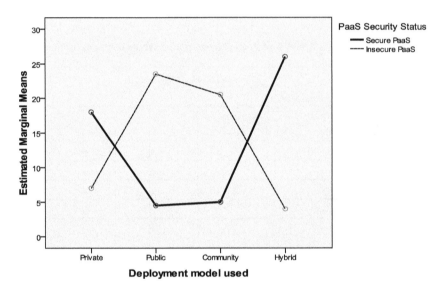

Figure 4.6(a): A graph depicting interaction effect between PaaS delivery model and cloud deployment models
Source:*Researcher*

4.7 IaaS delivery model versus cloud deployment models
Finally, IaaS data obtained from descriptive statistics results were recorded appropriately in SPSS version 19.0 and factorial analysis computed. The results generated are Factorial ANOVA table which contains F-value used to reject or accept null hypothesis based on 5% level of significance and factorial graph to check if there is any interaction effect between levels of main factors.

Table 4.7(a): Between-Subjects factors IaaS levels

Between-Subjects Factors			
		Value Label	N
IaaS Security Status	1	Secure IaaS	8
	2	Insecure IaaS	8
Deployment model used	1	Private	4
	2	Public	4
	3	Community	4
	4	Hybrid	4

Source: *Researcher*

Table 4.7(b): ANOVA of IaaS delivery model versus deployment model used

Tests of Between-Subjects Effects					
Dependent Variable:Replication					
Source	Type III Sum of Squares	df	Mean Square	F	Sig.
Corrected Model	992.438[a]	7	141.777	2.308	.132
Intercept	2475.062	1	2475.062	40.286	.000
IaaS_Status	.062	1	.062	.001	.975
DeploymentModel	27.188	3	9.063	.148	.928
IaaS_Status * DeploymentModel	965.188	3	321.729	5.237	.027
Error	491.500	8	61.438		
Total	3959.000	16			
Corrected Total	1483.938	15			
a. R Squared = .669 (Adjusted R Squared = .379)					

Source: *Researcher*

Table 4.7 (b) above shows Iaas Factorial ANOVA results and the tabulated outcome also indicates the interaction between the main effects deployment model * IaaS status (F=5.237, p = .027).

Furthermore, Figure 4.8(a) below, depicts a high interaction effect between of main factors (Iaas delivery model and deployment models). The resultant graph also strengthens the interaction effects between aforementioned main factors . As can be seen from the graph, private cloud is the safest cloud to deploy IaaS services, whereas public and community clouds are very insecure clouds as far as IaaS service delivery in the cloud is concerned.

Since the P-values for main interaction effects between deployment models and Saas security status effects are (F=5.237, p = .027<0.05), we reject H_0 at 5% level of significance and conclude that IaaS service delivery model and their respective deployment models used have significant effect on cloud computing security in the selected firms in Kenya.

Estimated Marginal Means of Replication

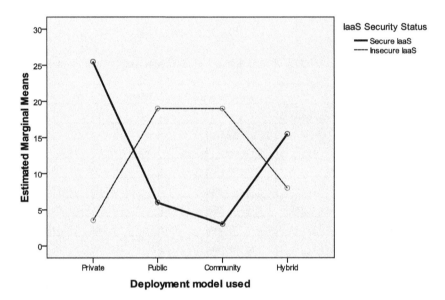

Figure 4.7(a): A graph depicting interaction effect between IaaS delivery model and cloud deployment models.
Source:*Researcher*

54

CHAPTER FIVE
SUMMARY, CONCLUSION AND RECOMMENDATIONS.

5.1 Summary.

The study was done in two selected cloud computing companies in Kenya namely the IonaCloud and KenyanCloud companies. The purpose of this study was concerned with investigation of security concerns of cloud computing service delivery models in selected companies in Kenya.

Chapter one provided the background information to the study, an overview of factors(variables) that have considerable impact on security concerns in cloud computing but have hitherto not been researched. The chapter also expressed the view that the researcher pin-pointed as the security concerns of cloud computing notably on service delivery model with their respective deployment models and the need to critically take in-depth analysis using a statistical model. It was on the basis of this background that the statement of the problem was stated, objectives and significance of the study outlined. Test of hypothesis, justification of the study and the definition of terms were also highlighted.

Chapter two highlighted literature reviews from authors who have researched on various cloud computing security concerns. The chapter singled out a researchable niche that has hitherto not been studied as far as cloud computing is concerned.

Chapter three was concerned with the methodology employed in this study. Factorial design was used to tabulate and present the findings. In particular, a 2x4 Factorial design.

In chapter four, primary data collected using questionnaires and interview were analyzed using SPSS version 19.0. Both descriptive statistics consisting of frequency tables and charts and inferential statistics, specifically factorial ANOVA tables and their corresponding main effects interaction graphs were used in the analysis to report and present the findings.

5.2 Discussion of the findings

As mentioned elsewhere in this book, the main objective of the study was to compare the security concerns of cloud computing service delivery models in selected firms in Kenya. In particular, the study sought to attain the specific objectives and theses that are discussed below. The first specific objective of the study was to answer *to establish whether SaaS service delivery model and the respective deployment models used have a significant effect on cloud computing security in the selected firms in Kenya.*

In quest of answering the above objective, respondents were fronted with pertinent questions to give their reactions as to whether SaaS services delivered on various cloud deployment models namely the private, public, community and hybrid clouds are all safe.

Regarding SaaS delivery model, the study findings pointed out that there is a significant effect on the type of deployment model used to host SaaS services in the cloud. In Particular, 72.73% of technicians from IonaCloud and 54.55% of technicians from KenyanCloud attested that SaaS services delivered on private cloud are always safe against 27.27% of technicians from the two companies who equally disagreed in the same proportion that private cloud is not always a safe cloud model to deploy SaaS services. A similar pattern of the results were exhibited by clients where 88.89% of clients from IonaCloud and 375.00% of clients from KenyanCloud concurred that private clouds are safest models to deploy and deliver SaaS services. These results concur with Spreeuwenberg (2012) that the hardware for the private cloud can be located on-premise or in a data center of the vendor. The advantage of this model is that an organization has total control over the hardware and that the organization has to worry less about the security since no other organizations are using the hardware. As to whether deploying SaaS services in public cloud was safe, 72.72% of technicians from IonaCloud an 45.46% of technicians from KenyanCloud were of the contrary opinion that public cloud is not the safest cloud to host and deliver SaaS services. The large margin disparity in response by technicians of the two companies can be attributed to the fact IonaCloud company is a little bit older as a service provider and therefore more experienced in cloud computing security concerns in both the deployment and delivery models. Moreover, when similar question was posed to the clients of the two companies and 77.78% of clients from IonaCloud and 50.00% clients from KenyanCloud, just like technicians also had low opinion on the safeness of both public deployment cloud as model of deployment SaaS services in the cloud. Another significant results pertaining community cloud vis-à-vis SaaS delivery model revealed that equal proportion of 54.55% of technicians from IonaCloud KenyanCloud disagreed to the fact SaaS data deployed on community cloud is safe, likewise to two companies' clients where 77.78% and 2(50.00%) of clients from IonaCloud and KenyanCloud respectively also had similar opinion to their technicians counterparts. As a backup to the deployment and delivery models, supplementary questions were posed to clients to give their feelings with regard to SaaS delivery model. Results indicated that 69.70% of technicians from IonaCloud and 81.82% of technicians from KenyanCloud disagreed to the fact that data or information on transit always safe regardless of the deployment model employed. This alone indicates not all deployment models are safe to host SaaS services and therefore requires further investigation. When asked as to whether, some deployment models allows unauthorized access to data/information in their cloud in SaaS delivery model, 51.52% of technicians from IonaCloud had low opinion whereas an overwhelming 81.82% of technicians from KenyanCloud equally disagreed. Nonetheless, 51.52% of technicians from IonaCloud and a paltry of 36.36% of technicians from Kenyan Cloud supported the fact that SaaS is vulnerable for improper access control, virtual machines operating systems flaws, cookies and hidden field manipulation as well as insecure storages and configurations as well as to the fact that hackers can manipulate weakness in data security model to get an illegitimate access to data or application. Finally, as to whether hackers can manipulate weaknesses in SaaS model to get illegitimate access to data/information, 75.76% of technicians from IonaCloud and 72.73% of technicians from KenyanCloud strongly defending their systems and disagreeing vehemently.

In order to ensure the consistency of results and establish the absence or presence of correlations between Security concerns in SaaS delivery model and deployment models, a test of hypothesis was formulated and test. The hypothesis formulated was: *SaaS service delivery model and the respective deployment models used have no significant effect on cloud computing security in the selected firms in Kenya.*

The findings revealed that there was significant difference((F=4.465, p = .040) interaction effect between the deployment model and SaaS delivery hence the null hypothesis was rejected and accept the alternative at 5% level of significance and conclude SaaS service delivery model and the respective deployment models used have significant effect on cloud computing security in the selected firms in Kenya. Results further uncovered that SaaS services deployed on community cloud are highly insecure whereas SaaS services deployed on either private, public and hybrid clouds were equally secure. In a nutshell, the overall results indicated the SaaS delivery model is dependent on the type of deployment model used to host and deliver its services in the cloud. In Particular, it is safe to host SaaS services in private, hybrid and community cloud.

The second specific objective of the study was *to establish whether PaaS service delivery model and the respective deployment models used have a significant effect on cloud computing security in the selected firms in Kenya.*

In quest of answering the second objective mentioned above, results showed that 87.87% of technicians from IonaCloud and 63.63% of technicians from KenyanCloud assented that PaaS services deployed on private cloud are always safe, while a paltry 30.30% and 18.18% of technicians from IonaCloud and KenyanCloud respectively similarly concurred that PaaS services hosted on public cloud are safe leaving out the majority of 69.70% technicians from IonaCloud and 81.82% vehemently disagreeing. Similarly, 77.78% of clients from IonaCloud and a whooping 100.00% of clients strongly attested to the fact that the most preferred deployment model for hosting PaaS services was the cloud. However, as opposed to SaaS model, 50.00% of the KenyanCloud clients and 55.56% of IonaCloud clients had low opinion on the safety of hybrid cloud when used to deploy PaaS services on the cloud. A similar and more resounding pattern for the least popular clouds in terms of safety was also found to be public cloud with 77.78% of clients from IonaCloud and 75.00% of clients from KenyanCloud having low opinion. However, a contrasting results were exhibited in technicians opinions towards PaaS being deployed in community cloud whereby whereas 75.76% of technicians from IonaCloud disagreed, there was a sharp contrast in response from KenyanCloud technicians where 63.63% assented that community cloud was safe for deploying and delivering PaaS services. However, 33.33% of clients from IonaCloud and 25.00%

of clients from KenyanCloud mildly agreed that community cloud could be the safest model for deploying PaaS services on the cloud. Just like in SaaS delivery model, the results in PaaS also revealed that most respondents, up to 81.82% technicians from IonaCloud and 54.55% of technicians KenyanCloud apparently agreed that hybrid cloud is a safe platform for hosting and deploying PaaS services. In conclusion, the results community and public clouds has highly insecure deployment models and hybrid cloud being the highly secure model for deploying PaaS services while private cloud fairly secure cloud for deploying PaaS services.

Besides answering the second research regarding security concerns in PaaS delivery model and deployment models, a test of hypothesis was formulated too. The hypothesis formulated was:

PaaS service delivery model and the respective deployment models used have no significant effect on cloud computing security in the selected firms in Kenya.

Upon testing the above hypothesis, research outcome indicated that was an significant difference between the main effects namely the deployment model and PaaS delivery model with results of (F=4.469, p = .040), hence, the null hypothesis was rejected and accept the alternative hypothesis. A conclusion was made that PaaS service delivery model and the respective deployment models used have significant effect on cloud computing security in the selected firms in Kenya. Moreover, the results inferences gave more insight on deployment models that befit the PaaS delivery model. The results discovered that PaaS services deployed on community and public clouds are highly insecure whereas hybrid cloud is highly secure model for deploying PaaS services than private cloud, although both are considerably secure clouds.

The third and final objective also sought *to establish whether IaaS service delivery model and the respective deployment models used have a significant effect on cloud computing security in the selected firms in Kenya.*

Responses of participants in the study indicated that 93.94% of technicians from IonaCloud and 72.73% of technicians from KenyanCloud vehemently agreed that private cloud is safe to host IaaS services in cloud. Analogous results was also exhibited by clients with 88.89% clients from IonaCloud and 75.00% clients from KenyanCloud also attested that the safest cloud for deploying IaaS services is private cloud. Public deployment model. With regards to public and community and clouds, almost similar responses were registered with 78.79% and 72.73% as well as 57.58% and 54.55% both from IonaCloud and KenyanCloud respectively disagreeing that both the public and community deployment models are not safe in deploying IaaS services in the cloud, although a considerable number of respondents were not sure about the safety of these two aforementioned deployment models. Likewise, there was very low opinion on safeness of public cloud with 77.78% from IonaCloud clients and 75.00% from KenyanCloud clients disagreeing to its safety. Nevertheless, 50.00% of clients from KenyanCloud agreed that community cloud was safe to deploy IaaS services in the cloud. However, a substantial number 63.64% of technicians at KenyanCloud supported the idea that hybrid cloud was a Safe cloud to deploy IaaS services but not for respondents from IonaCloud who registered a paltry of 39.39% also concurring with safety of the hybrid cloud being a better option to deploy IaaS services. Lastly, 66.67% of clients from IonaCloud agreed that hybrid cloud is secure to deploy IaaS services.

On Summative questions that were solely directed to technicians, 69.70% of technicians from IonaCloud aand 54.55% clients from KenyanCloud disapproved that the security of virtual machines (VM) boundaries that in the event that the company misconfigures or mismanage whether it could lead to unauthorized access and data leaks regardless of deployment model used. As to whether a closely related VM issues such as memory leaks, VM images attacks from malicious injection codes, risk of re-using VM templates and hypervisor weaknesses 54.55% technicians from IonaCloud and 63.64% of technicians from KenyanCloud disagree too that malware, DOS and memory leaks are most common threats regardless of deployment used in IaaS services. On the contrary, 66.67% of technicians from IonaCloud and 72.73% of technicians from KenyanCloud agreed that when VM templates are used as rapid deployment system, they may contain the original owner information might be re-used for new customers hence posing a security risk in IaaS platform. However, 93.94% of technicians from IonaCloud and a whooping 100.00% technicians from KenyanCloud disagreed to the fact that any vulnerability in hypervisor software usually inherits security risks in customer VMs. It was also revealed through results that while 72.73% of technicians from IonaCloud agreed that storage of data/Information and applications locations in IaaS delivery model are always safe regardless of the deployment model used, 54.55% of their counterparts at KenyanCloud of were of the contrary opinion.

In a nutshell, in IaaS delivery model, it was discovered that as opposed to SaaS and PaaS preferred clouds, the private cloud is the safest and trustworthy cloud to deploy IaaS over cloud. The hybrid cloud came second though a distant far from private cloud. It was further revealed that public and community clouds are equally risk models for deploying IaaS.

Finally, a test of hypothesis emanating from the third and final research objective was formulated and tested.. The test hypothesis formulated was:
IaaS service delivery model and the respective deployment models used have no significant effect on cloud computing security in the selected firms in Kenya.

The research outcome clearly showed that there was a significant difference in the main effects namely the deployment model and IaaS status which yielded the results (F=5.237, p = .027) due to interaction effect. This led to conclusion of rejecting the null hypothesis at 5% level of significance and make inference that IaaS service delivery model and the respective deployment models used have significant effect on cloud computing security in the selected firms in Kenya. Related results showed that private cloud is the safest cloud to deploy IaaS services, whereas public and community clouds are very insecure clouds as far as IaaS service delivery in the cloud is concerned.

In a nutshell, a general summary of the data findings indicated that the service delivery models namely the SaaS, PaaS and IaaS have a significant effect on the type of deployment model(private, public, community or hybrid clouds) used.

5.3 Conclusion
The findings of the study have indicated that the kind of deployment model used as a mode of provisioning the cloud computing delivery models matters a lot because it has a considerable impact on the security concerns. There exist a relationships and dependencies between the three service delivery models such that PaaS as well as SaaS are hosted on top of IaaS; thus, any breach in IaaS will impact the security of

both PaaS and SaaS services, but also it may be true on the other way around. However, we have to take into account that PaaS offers a platform to build and deploy SaaS applications, which increases the security dependency between them. As a consequence of these deep dependencies, any attack to any cloud service layer can compromise the upper layers. Each cloud service model comprises its own inherent security flaws; however, they also share some challenges that affect all of them. These relationships and dependencies between cloud models may also be a source of security risks. A SaaS provider may rent a development environment from a PaaS provider, which might also rent an infrastructure from an IaaS provider. Each provider is responsible for securing his own services, which may result in an inconsistent combination of security models. It also creates confusion over which service provider is responsible once an attack happens.

Cloud computing security concerns has always been there right from the inception of internet and networking. The companies offering cloud computing services here in Kenya are aware of the risks but not from this perspective. In spite of that, high security measures have been put in place to curb the rampant risks in the cloud. The trend in cloud computing is rapidly and dynamically undergoing various improvements from various players and stakeholders. The study, however found out that the technical personnel of cloud providers organizations play a bigger role as far as cloud services are concerned. The activities of the clients also exerts a considerable influence on the service providers in provision and unprovisioning the cloud computing services. Recommendations made in the study are hoped that they will assist to minimize risks involved when choosing and deploying cloud computing services. Motivated by the need to better understanding the incentives of the user's trust in cloud computing, the four deployment models namely the private, public, community and hybrid versus service delivery models namely the SaaS, PaaS and IaaS were interactively analyzed. Regarding these models, theoretical perspectives of trust have been synthesized and a model for consumer trust in cloud computing is developed. Analyzing the interactive effects of these models, trust was investigated and described. The outcomes of this book could be a clue to better recognizing the main parameters affecting users trust and characterizing each parameter's importance.

5.4 Recommendations

The following recommendations were reached from the study;

Having looked at the findings of security concerns on the type of service delibvery model vis-à-vis the type of deployment model used, the study recommends the following;-

(i)   The cloud computing service provider and the clients must make sure that the cloud is safe from all the external threats and there must be a mutual understanding between the client and the provider when it comes to the security on Cloud.

(ii)   Before choosing the service delivery model, it is imperative to also decide the type of deployment model one should use in the cloud.

(iii) Besides private cloud, clients should embrace hybrid deployment model because it leverages the advantage of the other cloud models, providing a more optimal user experience.

(iv)   The factorial design approach of analyzing cloud computing security will give an insight providers who will come up with a new model of delivering and deploying cloud computing services to clients. The model should offer enhanced choice, flexibility, operational efficiency and safety of the customer.

5.7 Areas of further Research

This study exclusively explored security concerns of service delivery model when deployed in different cloud, but there are a numerous (almost infinite) security risks associated with the cloud computing procedure and process. Hence, the following areas requires further research.

1. Security concerns in service delivery models with their respective deployments models in large Cloud computing provider organizations like Amazon's

2. The impact of security concerns that exist in relationship and dependencies between SaaS, PaaS and IaaS

3. Security concerns in private, public, community and hybrid deployment models

REFERENCES

Aron, S.H.(1986). *Test, Measurement, Research Methods in Behavioural Science.* New Delhi: McGraw Hill.

Balasubramanian R., Aramudhan, M.(2012). Security Issues: Public vs Private vs Hybrid Cloud Computing. *International Journal of Computer Applications* Volume 55 (0975 – 8887), p 13. Retrieved on 12th October, 2012 from http://research.ijcaonline.org/volume55/number13/pxc3882808.pdf

Bhadauria et al., (2012). *A Survey on Security Issues in Cloud Computing.* Vellore Institute of Technology, Vellore, India

Boss, G., Malladi, P., Quan, D., Legregni, L., & Hall, H. (2007). *Cloud Computing.* Retrieved on 20th May, 2012, from ww.ibm.com/developerwork/websphere/zones/hipods

Brodkin, J. (2008). *Seven cloud-computing security risks.* Retrieved September 12, 2012, from http://www.infoworld.com/d/security-central/gartner-seven-cloud- computing-security-risks-853

CCIA (2009). Abstract*: Cloud Computing, Computer & Communications Industry Association.* Retrieved on August 30, 2012 from http:// www.ccianet.org/CCIA/files/ccLibraryFiles/Filename/ 000000000151/Cloud_Computing.pdf

Cronbach, L.J.(1951). Coefficient alpha and the internal structure of tests. *Psychometrika,* pp 297 – 334.

Datapipe (2010). *The Dollars and Cents of Cloud Computing.* Retrieved on October 24, 2012 from http://blog.datapipe.com/cloud-computing-2/the-dollars-and-cents-of-cloud-computing/

Descher, M, Masser, P, Feilhauer, T, Tjoa, A.M, Huemer, D.(2009, March). *Retaining data control to the client in infrastructure clouds*: Paper presented in International conference on availability, reliability and security, ARES.

Dikaiakos, M. D., et al (2009). *Cloud Computing: Distributed Internet Computing for IT and Scientific Research. In IEEE Internet Computing,* September/October, 2009, Vol. 13, No. 5, pp. 10-13.

Hesse-Biber, S.N. (2010). *Mixed Methods Research.* Merging Theory with Practice. New York: The Guilford Press.

Kandukuri, B.R, Paturi, V.R, Rakshit , A.(2009, March). *Cloud security issues*: IEEE international conference on services computing, Tirunelveli, India.

Kajiyama, T. (2012). *Cloud Computing Security: How Risks and Threats Ar Affecting Cloud Adoption Decisions.* Unpublished Thesis, San Diego State University.

Kerlinger, F.N. (1986). *Foundations of Behavioural Research.* New York: Subject Publishers.

Kombo, D.K. and Tromp D.L.A.(2006). *Proposal and Thesis Writing, an Introduction,* Nairobi: Paulines Publishers.

Kothari C.R. (2004). *Research Methodology, Methods and Techniques,* *(2nd ed.).* New Delhi: New Age International Publishers.

Mell, E, Grance, T.(2011). *The NIST definition of cloud computing.* November, 22 , 2012 from http://csrc.nist.gov/publications/nistpubs/800-145/SP800-145.pdf

Morsy A. M., Grundy J., Muller I.(2010). *An Analysis of The Cloud Computing Security Problem.* Retrieved October 25, 2012 from http://www.ict.swin.edu.au/personal/malmorsy/Pubs/ cloud2010_1.pdf

Mugenda, O., & Mugenda, A. (1999).*Research Methods.* Nairobi: ACIS Publishers.

NIST (2009). *The NIST Cloud Definition Framework.* Retrieved March 14th , 2011 from http://csrc.nist.gov/groups/SNS/cloud-computing/cloud-computing-v26.ppt

O'Neill M.(2010). *SaaS, PaaS, and IaaS: A security checklist for cloud models.* Retrieved On February 2, 2013, from http://www.csoonline.com/article/660065/saas-paas-and-iaas-a-security-checklist-for-cloud-models.htm

Patel B.D. (2011). *Design and Implementation of Business Expense Manager Software Application On Cloud Computing Environment.* Unpublished Master's project, California State University, Northridge.

Rehan, S.(2011). *Cloud computing's effect on enterprises.* Unpublished master's Thesis, Lund University.

Routio, P.(2007). *Comparative Study.* Retrieved on August 3rd , 2012 from http://www2.uiah.fi/projects/metodi

Savu, L.(2011).*Cloud Computing: Deployment Models, Delivery Models, Risks and Research Challenges.* Tirunelveli, IEEE.

Shinder T.W. (2011, August 3). Security Issues in Cloud Deployment model. *TechNet Articles*, p. 2. Retrived on August 3rd , 2012 from http://social.technet.microsoft.com/wiki/contents/articles/ security-issues-in-cloud-deployment-models.aspx from TechNet database.

Smith, L. (2011). *Advice for dealing with the top 10 risks in public cloud computing.* Retrieved September 27, 2012 from http://searchcio.techtarget.com/news/2240031598/Advice-for-dealing-with-the-top-10-risks-in-public-cloud-computing

Spreeuwenberg, M.(2012). *Cloud Computing.* Unpublished Master's Thesis, Radboud University, Nijmegen.

Subra K. (2011). *Introduction to Cloud Security Architecture from a Cloud Consumer's Perspective.* Anna University Tirunelveli, Tirunelveli

Subashini S, Kavitha V(2010). A survey on security issues in service delivery models of cloud computing. *Journal of Network and Computer Applications,* volume 2, (Issue 5), p. 3-4. Retrived on 14th December, 2012, from www.doi:10.1016/j.jnca.2010.07.006

Tech Mtaa. (2011) *Cloud Computing Takes Centre Stage In Kenya.* . Retrieved on July 4, 2012 from http:// www.techmtaa.com/2011/01/06/cloud-computin-takes-centre-stage-in-kenya/

Thibodeau, P. (2010). The Vapour 10 big cloud trends for 2010. *Computerworld.* Singapore. January-February 2010 issue, p 33

Yamane, T.(1967). *Sampling Statistics.* New Jersey(Englewood Cliffs): Prentice-Hall.

APPENDIX 4: Technicians 2x4 factorial design data on SaaS vs
Deployment models

APPENDIX 4(a):2x4 factorial design data on SaaS vs Deployment models

Delivery Model	Deployment models				
		Private	Public	Community	Hybrid
SaaS	1.Secure	29, 10	8, 6	4, 2	20, 12
	2. Insecure	10, 6	8, 8	29, 14	8, 3

APPENDIX 4(b):2x4 factorial design data on PaaS vs Deployment models

Delivery Model	Deployment models				
		Private	Public	Community	Hybrid
PaaS	1.Secure	25, 11	5, 4	8, 2	38, 14
	2. Insecure	8, 6	34, 13	27, 14	6, 2

APPENDIX 4(c):2x4 factorial design data on IaaS vs Deployment models

Delivery Model	Deployment models				
		Private	Public	Community	Hybrid
IaaS	1.Secure	14, 14	29, 7	16, 4	29, 11
	2. Insecure	30, 3	14, 9	19, 13	15, 4

APPENDIX 5: Clients 2x4 factorial design data on SaaS vs Deployment models

APPENDIX 5(a):2x4 factorial design data on SaaS vs Deployment models

Delivery Model		Deployment models			
		Private	Public	Community	Hybrid
SaaS	1.Secure	8, 3	2, 1	1, 1	5, 2
	2. Insecure	1, 1	5, 3	7, 2	2, 1

APPENDIX 5(b):2x4 factorial design data on PaaS vs Deployment models

Delivery Model		Deployment models			
		Private	Public	Community	Hybrid
PaaS	1.Secure	7, 4	2, 0	3, 1	3, 1
	2. Insecure	1, 0	7, 3	4, 2	5, 2

APPENDIX 5(c):2x4 factorial design data on IaaS vs Deployment models

Delivery Model		Deployment models			
		Private	Public	Community	Hybrid
IaaS	1.Secure	8, 3	1, 0	1, 2	6, 2
	2. Insecure	1, 1	7, 3	6, 2	2, 2

APPENDIX 6: Intercept, Corrected model and Total

The "**intercept**" is what most textbooks (especially older ones) call the "**correction factor(cf).**" It is the grand total squared divided by N. (Equivalently, it is xbar squared times sqrt(N).

The "**Corrected total**" is what we call the total sum of squares (tss-cf).

The "**total**" is the total sum of squares before you subtract the correction factor, or, equivalently, sigma(X-squared).

The "**corrected model**" is, when you have equal sample sizes, the sum of the main effects and the interaction. When you don't have equal sample sizes, it is the variability that can be explained by all three effects (the two main effects and the interaction) simultaneously.

APPENDIX 7: Reliability of Technicians' data collection Instrument

Reliability Statistics	
Cronbach's Alpha	N of Items
.664	34

APPENDIX 8: Reliability of Clients data collection Instrument

Reliability Statistics		
Cronbach's Alpha	Cronbach's Alpha Based on Standardized Items	N of Items
.770	.742	18